ESSAYS
Thought and Style

Brian Kellow   John Krisak

Prentice-Hall Canada Inc.
Scarborough, Ontario

Canadian Cataloguing in Publication Data

Main entry under title:

Essays: thought and style

For use in high schools.
ISBN 0-13-283573-8

1. English language—Style. 2. English language—Rhetoric.
3. American essays—20th century.
I. Kellow, Brian, II. Krisak, John.

PE1421.E88 1987   808'.4   C87-093192-X

Prentice-Hall, Inc., Englewood Cliffs, New Jersey
Prentice-Hall International, Inc., London
Prentice-Hall of Australia, Pty., Ltd., Sydney
Prentice-Hall of India Pvt., Ltd., New Delhi
Prentice-Hall of Japan, Inc., Tokyo
Prentice-Hall of Southeast Asia (PTE) Ltd., Singapore
Editora Prentice-Hall do Brasil Ltda., Rio de Janeiro
Prentice-Hall Hispanoamericana, S.A., Mexico

   3 4 5 6 W 92 91 90 89 88

Printed and bound in Canada by Webcom

Project Editor: Paula Pettitt
Production Editor: Brian Day
Production: Irene Maunder
Design: Bruce Bond
Composition: Attic Typesetting Inc.
Cover: HARRIS, Lawren S.
       Canadian (1885–1970)
       Clouds. Lake Superior, 1923. Oil on canvas; 111.5 × 136.3 cm.
       Collection of The Winnipeg Art Gallery.
       Donated by John A. MacAulay, Q.C.
       Photography: The Winnipeg Art Gallery, Ernest P. Mayer
       Courtesy of the family of Lawren S. Harris

CONTENTS

Writing to Persuade   127

Writing to Reflect   149

Writing to Enthrall   185

Acknowledgements

This project has been enriched by the support of many people—colleagues, friends and family whose help we would now like to formally acknowledge. Special thanks are also extended to the following people at Prentice-Hall Canada Inc. whose contributions to this book have been extensive and with whom we have worked so closely—David Steele, Paula Pettitt, Brian Day, Irene Maunder and Bruce Bond.

John Krisak
Brian Kellow

For Rebecca, Rachel, Sarah, Geoffrey, Brian and David.

Preface

A fine essay expresses interesting thought in an engaging style. The thought can be on any subject; the style can be daring or restrained. In the excellent essay, the reader hears the authentic voice of the practised and confident writer.

The essays in this collection deal with subjects ranging from the influence of pop music to the genius of Shakespeare; from microbiology to thunderstorms; from love to computer technology; from piano lessons to the basketball court. Essays which contain generic language are balanced by those which attack the use of such language. This range of subjects and diversity of approaches provides some indication of the adaptability of the essay genre.

The essays in this collection are grouped according to purposes for writing. Some essays argue a point of view while others define, describe, explain or rhapsodize. The alternative listing of contents, at the back of the book, arranges the essays by theme and by form.

The study questions and assignments are designed to illuminate both the thought and style of each essay. Pre-Reading questions establish the context for the ideas of the essay by engaging students in their own ideas and observations. Thought questions help students develop their abilities to describe, summarize, analyze and evaluate the ideas in the essays. Style and Structure questions direct students to examine the language, sentence structure and organization, and also ask them to identify the purpose, audience and point of view of each essay. Response and Extension activities encourage students to respond personally, critically and creatively to the essays. Unit Synthesis activities at the end of each unit include comparison/contrast questions that ask students to examine essays in this collection and/or other works, as well as suggestions for comprehensive independent study projects.

Some of our favourite writers are here. We are envious of you who are discovering them for the first time.

John Krisak
Brian Kellow

WRITING TO OBSERVE

"The tolerance for a high decibel rate, masquerading as 'music', is in my opinion inversely proportional to the level of intelligence." So observes, and comments, Sydney J. Harris in his essay, "Blasting Music to Drown Out Reality." A specific observation has led him to write a general comment.

When Harry Bruce writes, "Of all holidays, Labour Day is the one that makes you grow up," his intention is not so much to convince as to express an opinion. His essay presents impressions, not totalities. It is enough that *he* is convinced.

Gloria Steinem's comment, "Planning ahead is a measure of class," was formulated after she observed the manner in which various people manage their time.

"The trouble is, our leaders have not adequately prepared us for a mechanized society," observes Woody Allen. "Unfortunately our politicians are either incompetent or corrupt," he comments. "Sometimes both on the same day."

These four voices, ranging from the calm and insightful to the whimsical and absurd, all present aphoristic comments on human behaviour. Each essay contains a moment of surprise or discovery which illuminates the diversity of human experience.

Labour Day Is a Dreaded Bell in the Schoolyard of the Mind

Harry Bruce

- What signals the end of summer for you?
- How is Labour Day different from other holidays for you?

Labour Day was like a sniff of the woods or a glimpse of the sea before they led you down to the dungeon. All other statutory holidays were an escape from school. Labour Day was its entrance, the stairway to an aeon of misery, a last meal, a last drag on a cigarette. At a cabin on a widening of the dark Magnetawan River, I'd sometimes smell Labour Day's deadly gloom as early as mid-August. While birch crackled in the kitchen stove and pancakes sizzled at breakfast, while I played rummy by coal-oil lantern or knocked about in a leaky punt under singing trees, while I routed the evil sheriff in my own Sherwood Forest, and even as I lifted a forkful of home-made raspberry pie to my mouth, a cold bell might ring in the far schoolyard of my mind. It was a signal. Now, Labour Day was yawning, getting to its feet, slouching toward me. It would take me back. All this would end.

I hated school. If Tom Hansen, 24, of Boulder, Colorado, wins his $350,000-suit against his mother and father for ruining his life with "psychological malparenting," I'm going to hit the Toronto education authorities for the psychological malteaching they put me through. School was hot, degrading, boring and occasionally terrifying, a house of despair in which big tyrants tormented small victims. The teachers, like prison guards, knew society wanted their institutions to be unpleasant for us inmates; and the worst punishment they could inflict, next to The Strap, was a "detention." It was an order to do extra time in the hole (school).

The vocabulary of discipline and insult, the smell of chalk and ink and old chewing gum, the feel of the hardwood bench under your haunches, the sickening realization that things would be this way till the end of an inconceivably distant June...all these awaited us on the morning after going to bed on Labour Day. After Christmas, kids asked one another, "Wud ya get?" After Labour Day, they asked, "*Who'd* ya get?" I'd say, "Mr. Such-and-such" or "Miss So-and-so." In a cruel flash, I'd learned the name and scowl of the adult who would dominate my daylight hours for ten months to come; and the other kid always replied, "You poor sucker."

Good morning, Miss Authoritarian. Good-bye, bonfires on the beach. Hello there, line-ups, marching in columns of two, standing stiffly at attention, sitting with your hands folded on your desk, keeping your trap shut. Good-bye picnics on the flat, sun-baked stone of deserted islands, good-bye blackberry bushes in bee-loud glades. Hello, scribbler and ruler. Good-bye, cry of the loon, depredations of the racoon, sunburn at noon, and hide-and-seek by the light of the moon. Good morning, *sir*.

There's another side to the Labour Day story, of course. Sadly, slowly, as though he were savoring the last moments of our crashing shore in Nova Scotia, an old friend from Toronto folded his tent, loaded his van. The Labour Day weekend had started, and he had 1,300 miles to drive. "Why not stick around a few days?" I said. "Can't," he grunted. "Got to be in class Tuesday morning." My friend is a high-school teacher. "Jeez, I hate Labour Day," he said, and rumbled out of my life for a few more seasons.

Labour Day is the prelude to work, and the death of play. Down at the Canadian National Exhibition, the unions are on parade. Out around the country, traffic fatalities mount. Thousands of family cars mournfully crawl away from wilderness retreats to city duties. Thousands of guitars, hibachis, sleeping bags, bathing suits, car-top boats, golf clubs and fishing poles are city-bound. Thousands of young lovers wonder if, ever again in another summer, they'll see the golden partners with whom they've recently lost their virginity. Will he, or she, really write? Can a fair-weather romance survive the killer winter? Camps close, and board up the season. Hotels cut their rates, and banish staff. Is that tree dead, or is it just that its leaves have already begun to turn? The chestnuts ripen. The days are shorter, and the nights cooler. Labour Day is a bummer.

Earlier than I needed to know, it taught me that no summer ever repeats itself, friendships must die, good times must always end, and the years melt people and beloved places. Of all holidays, Labour Day is the one that makes you grow up. And feel old. Nowadays, I dislike it more than ever.

Thought

1. With which of the images of Labour Day in the essay do you most strongly identify? Explain.
2. Compare your feelings about school with Harry Bruce's.
3. Did the author's anecdote about his friend the teacher surprise you? Explain.
4. What has Labour Day taught the author?

Style and Structure

5. Is the opening sentence appropriate for setting the tone of the essay? Explain.
6. Select three sentences from the body of the essay which are consistent in tone with the opening sentence.
7. Show how Bruce makes effective use of contrast in the fourth paragraph.
8. In what ways does the tone of the conclusion contrast with that of the introduction?
9. Select three of the author's observations and show how they lead directly to his final comments.

Response and Extension

10. Write a letter to yourself explaining how this school year will be different from all previous years. Seal the letter in an envelope and do not open it until the last day of class.
11. Using Bruce's essay as your model, write about a holiday of your choice, dealing with your negative and/or positive feelings towards this holiday.

Blasting Music to Drown Out Reality

Sydney J. Harris

- What is music?
- What are the purposes of music? Why do people create and listen to music?
- Do you think music ever becomes noise? If so, when?

The contractor sent around two sullen, slack-jawed young assistants to do some repair work on the tennis court across the road. They brought with them, inevitably, as standard equipment for the job, a powerful portable radio which kept blasting away for a full afternoon.

Call me any ugly word you will, such as snobbish or elitist, it remains my firm and unshakeable opinion that such people are as close to the moronic line as it is possible to get and still function in a social order. The tolerance for a high decibel rate, masquerading as "music," is in my opinion inversely proportional to the level of intelligence.

I can understand the need for what my children call elevator music in some factories or even restaurants, to keep the help from falling asleep or brooding on the essential monotony of their jobs. It is less pardonable in dentists' offices and such, but there it is at least relatively soft and easily ignored.

But these young men are working in August among grass and flowers and birds and birch trees, with a lovely view of the water and the cliffs and everything you might want to feast your senses on; instead, they anesthetized themselves with the junkiest of junk music throughout this God-given afternoon in a serenely sylvan setting.

My own theory is that people such as that turn on the radio not to bring something in, but to shut something out. It is not in order to hear the music, but in order that the vacuum in their minds may be soothed by sound, so that silence does not force them into thinking about themselves or experiencing the real world of perception and sensation.

And basically, what they want to shut out is the reality of their existence. This urge, almost a compulsion, to keep reality at arm's length is nearly pandemic in our society. It accounts not only for the incessant, frenetic music, but also for the drugs, the booze, the sports mania, the television addiction, the intense preoccupation with trivia—all of which act as opiates, dulling any sense of reality.

Marx's harsh dictum of the last century can almost be turned upside down today to read: "Opium is the religion of the people." And nowhere—not even in drugs or booze—can this be more clearly seen than in the kind of music spewing forth from portables and automobile radios and most hi-fi sets.

Music began as a celebration of nature and an exploration of the human spirit. Bach elevates us, Mozart delights us, Beethoven deepens us; all bring us closer to the wellsprings of life. Now this great gift has been turned against itself, blasting forth a cacophony to dull and deaden and dehumanize the soul.

Thought

1. What is the thesis of the essay?
2. Does the author support his thesis convincingly? Explain.
3. Does the conclusion proceed logically from the argument? Explain.

Style and Structure

4. Show how the author's diction betrays his bias.
5. Quote two sentences which are judgemental. Explain how they are judgemental.
6. To whom does Harris direct his comments? Explain.

Response and Extension

7. In groups, discuss the importance that you attach to the following: music, silence, thought, order, boredom. Develop a short audio-visual presentation as a summary of the observations and comments from your discussion.

8. (a) Develop a thesis based upon your observations on the relation of
   i) portable radios and tape players with headphones,
   ii) radios and tape players used in public places without headphones

   to issues of
   iii) personal space,
   iv) public space,
   v) individual rights,
   vi) collective rights.

   (b) Write a personal essay which develops this thesis.

9. Choose one of the composers Harris mentions. Present a short biography of the composer with examples of his music.

The Time Factor

Gloria Steinem

- How important is the present as it relates to your past and future?
- As a class, devise a list of those expressions which treat time as a commodity, e.g., "buying time," "I've got too much time on my hands."
- Discuss what these expressions reveal about the ways we perceive and use time.

Planning ahead is a measure of class. The rich and even the middle class plan for future generations, but the poor can plan ahead only a few weeks or days.

I remember finding this calm insight in some sociological text and feeling instant recognition. Yes, of course, our sense of time was partly a function of power, or the lack of it. It rang true even in the entirely economic sense the writer had in mind. "The guys who own the factories hand them down to their sons and great-grandsons," I remember a boy in my high school saying bitterly. "On this side of town, we just plan for Saturday night."

But it also seemed equally true of most of the women I knew—including myself—regardless of the class we supposedly belonged to. Though I had left my factory-working neighbourhood, gone to college, become a journalist, and thus was middle class, I still felt that I couldn't plan ahead. I had to be flexible—first, so that I could be ready to get on a plane for any writing assignment (even though the male writers I knew launched into books and other long-term projects on their own), and then so that I could adapt to the career and priorities of an eventual husband and children (even though I was leading a rewarding life without either). Among the results of this uncertainty were a stunning lack of career planning and such smaller penalties as no savings, no insurance, and an apartment that lacked basic pieces of furniture.

On the other hand, I had friends who were married to men whose long-term career plans were compatible with their own, yet they still lived their lives in day-to-day response to any possible needs of their husbands and children. Moreover, the one male colleague who shared or even understood this sense of powerlessness was a successful black journalist and literary critic who admitted that even after twenty years he planned only one assignment at a time. He couldn't forget his dependence on the approval of white editors.

Clearly there is more to this fear of the future than a conventional definition of class could explain. There is also caste: the unchangeable marks of sex and race that bring a whole constellation of cultural injunctions against power, even the limited power of controlling one's own life.

We haven't yet examined time-sense and future planning as functions of discrimination, but we have begun to struggle with them, consciously or not. As a movement, women have become painfully conscious of too much reaction and living from one emergency to the next, with too little initiative and planned action of our own; hence many of our losses to a much smaller but more entrenched and consistent right wing.

Though the cultural habit of living in the present and glazing over the future goes deep, we've begun to challenge the cultural punishment awaiting the "pushy" and "selfish" women (and the "uppity" minority men) who try to break through it and control their own lives.

Even so, feminist writers and theorists tend to avoid the future by lavishing all our analytical abilities on what's wrong with the present, or on revisions of history and critiques of the influential male thinkers of the past. The big, original, and certainly courageous books of this wave of feminism have been more diagnostic than prescriptive. We need pragmatic planners and visionary futurists, but can we think of even one feminist five-year-plan? Perhaps the closest we have come is visionary architecture or feminist science fiction, but they generally avoid the practical steps of how to get from here to there.

Obviously, many of us need to extend our time-sense—to have the courage to plan for the future, even while most of us are struggling to keep our heads above water in the present. But this does not mean a flat-out imitation of the culturally masculine habit of planning ahead, living in the future, and thus living a deferred life. It doesn't mean the traditional sacrifice of spontaneous action, or a sensitive awareness of the present, that comes from long years of career education with little intrusion of reality, from corporate pressure to work now for the sake of a reward after retirement, or, least logical of all, from patriarchal religions that expect obedience now in return for a reward after death.

In fact, the ability to live in the present, to tolerate uncertainty, and to remain open, spontaneous, and flexible are all culturally female qualities that many men need and have been denied. As usual, both halves of the polarized masculine-feminine division need to learn from each other's experiences. If men spent more time raising small children, for instance, they would be forced to develop more patience and flexibility. If women had more power in the planning of natural resources and other long-term processes—or even in the planning of our own careers and reproductive lives—we would have to develop more sense of the future and of cause and effect.

An obsession with reacting to the present, feminine-style, or on controlling and living in the future, masculine-style, are both wasteful of time.

And time is all there is.

Thought

1. According to Steinem, how do the following groups regard time: the poor; the rich; women; men? Do you agree or disagree with her observations?
2. What does Steinem mean by "the fear of the future"?
3. Examine the concept of "cultural punishment."
4. Evaluate the recommendations Steinem makes which would "extend our time-sense."

Style and Structure

5. Does Steinem betray a bias in her opening observations? Consider her diction and sentence structure.
6. At what point in the essay does Steinem move from thesis statement to thesis development? Explain.
7. Identify the audience Steinem has in mind for her essay.

Response and Extension

8. In groups, devise a questionnaire to poll people's perceptions of time based on Steinem's and your own observations. Administer your questionnaire to several people of various ages. Summarize your results and report them to the class.
9. Write an essay which examines the contention that control of one's time is control of one's life.

My Speech to the Graduates

Woody Allen

- List several serious matters about which people make jokes.
- Quote examples of this sort of joke.
- Why do some people make jokes about serious matters?

More than any other time in history, mankind faces a crossroads. One path leads to despair and utter hopelessness. The other, to total extinction. Let us pray we have the wisdom to choose correctly. I speak, by the way, not with any sense of futility, but with a panicky conviction of the absolute meaninglessness of existence which could easily be misinterpreted as pessimism. It is not. It is merely a healthy concern for the predicament of modern man. (Modern man is here defined as any person born after Nietzsche's edict that "God is dead," but before the hit recording "I Wanna Hold Your Hand.") This "predicament" can be stated one of two ways, though certain linguistic philosophers prefer to reduce it to a mathematical equation where it can be easily solved and even carried around in the wallet.

Put in its simplest form, the problem is: How is it possible to find meaning in a finite world given my waist and shirt size? This is a very difficult question when we realize that science has failed us. True, it has conquered many diseases, broken the genetic code, and even placed human beings on the moon, and yet when a man of eighty is left in a room with two eighteen-year-old cocktail waitresses nothing happens. Because the real problems never change. After all, can the human soul be glimpsed through a microscope? Maybe—but you'd definitely need one of those very good ones with two eyepieces. We know that the most advanced computer in the world does not have a brain as sophisticated as that of an ant. True, we could say that of many of our relatives but we only have to put up with them at weddings or special occasions. Science is something we depend on all the time. If I develop a pain in the chest I must take an X-ray. But what if the radiation from the X-ray causes me deeper problems? Before I know it, I'm going in for surgery. Naturally, while they're giving me oxygen an intern decides to light up a cigarette. The next thing you know I'm rocketing over the World Trade Center in bed clothes. Is this science? True, science has taught us how to pasteurize cheese. And true, this can be fun in mixed company—but what of the H-bomb? Have you ever seen what happens when one of those things falls off a desk accidentally? And where is science when one ponders the eternal riddles? How did the cosmos originate? How long has it been around? Did matter begin with an explosion or by the word of God? And if by the latter, could He not have begun it just two weeks earlier to take advantage of some of the warmer weather? Exactly what do we mean when we say, man is mortal? Obviously it's not a compliment.

Religion too has unfortunately let us down. Miguel de Unamuno writes blithely of the "eternal persistence of consciousness," but this is no easy feat. Particularly when reading Thackeray. I often think how comforting life must have been for early man because he believed in a powerful, benevolent Creator who looked after all things. Imagine his disappointment when he saw his wife putting on weight. Contemporary man, of course, has no such peace of mind. He finds himself in the midst of a crisis of faith. He is what we fashionably call "alienated." He has seen the ravages of war, he has known natural catastrophes, he has been to singles bars. My good friend Jacques Monod spoke often of the randomness of the cosmos. He believed everything in existence occurred by pure chance with the possible exception of his breakfast, which he felt certain was made by his housekeeper. Naturally belief in a divine intelligence inspires tranquillity. But this does not free us from our human responsibilities. Am I my brother's keeper? Yes. Interestingly, in my case I share that honor with the Prospect Park Zoo. Feeling godless then, what we have done is made technology God. And yet can technology really be the answer when a brand new Buick, driven by my close associate, Nat Zipsky, winds up in the window of Chicken Delight causing hundreds of customers to scatter? My toaster has never once worked properly in four years. I follow the instructions and push two slices of bread down in the slots and seconds later they rifle upward. Once they broke the nose of a woman I loved very dearly. Are we counting on nuts and bolts and electricity to solve our problems? Yes, the telephone is a good thing—and the refrigerator—and the air conditioner. But not every air conditioner. Not my sister Henny's, for instance. Hers makes a loud noise and still doesn't cool. When the man comes over to fix it, it gets worse. Either that or he tells her she needs a new one. When she complains, he says not to bother him. This man is truly alienated. Not only is he alienated but he can't stop smiling.

The trouble is, our leaders have not adequately prepared us for a mechanized society. Unfortunately our politicians are either incompetent or corrupt. Sometimes both on the same day. The Government is unresponsive to the needs of the little man. Under five-seven, it is impossible to get your Congressman on the phone. I am not denying that democracy is still the finest form of government. In a democracy at least, civil liberties are upheld. No citizen can be wantonly tortured, imprisoned, or made to sit through certain Broadway shows. And yet this is a far cry from what goes on in the Soviet Union. Under their form of totalitarianism, a person merely caught whistling is sentenced to thirty years in a labour camp. If, after fifteen years, he still will not stop whistling, they shoot him. Along with this brutal fascism we find its handmaiden, terrorism. At no other time in history has man been so afraid to cut into his veal chop for fear that it will explode. Violence breeds more violence and it is predicted that by 1990 kidnapping will be the dominant mode of social interaction. Overpopulation will exacerbate problems to the breaking point. Figures tell us there are already more people on earth than we need to move even the heaviest piano. If we do not call a halt to breeding, by the year 2000 there will be no room to serve dinner unless one is willing to set the table on the heads of strangers. Then they must not move for an hour while we eat. Of course energy will be in short supply and each car owner will be allowed only enough gasoline to back up a few inches.

Instead of facing these challenges we turn instead to distractions like drugs and sex. We live in far too permissive a society. Never before has pornography been this rampant. And those films are lit so badly! We are a people who lack defined goals. We have never learned to love. We lack leaders and coherent programs. We have no spiritual center. We are adrift alone in the cosmos wreaking monstrous violence on one another out of frustration and pain. Fortunately, we have not lost our sense of proportion. Summing up, it is clear the future holds great opportunities. It also holds pitfalls. The trick will be to avoid the pitfalls, seize the opportunities, and get back home by six o'clock.

Thought

1. According to Woody Allen, what is the "predicament" of modern humanity? What is your immediate response to the way in which he has stated this predicament? Explain.
2. Evaluate Allen's comments on the "failure" of science, religion, and politics.
3. In the author's opinion, what do we do instead of facing challenges? Do you agree? Why or why not?

Style and Structure

4. From the essay quote examples of: a) incongruity, b) exaggeration.
5. Closely examine one paragraph in which each device is used and explain why the effect is humorous.

Response and Extension

6. In groups, prepare a humorous speech on a serious subject. Select one member of your group to deliver the speech to the rest of the class.
7. Select a conventional situation in which speeches are given. Define the usual characteristics of the speech, taking into consideration the purpose and the audience. Write a parody of a conventional speech, using Allen's example as a model.

Unit Synthesis

1. Read several columns by well-known syndicated newspaper columnists, such as Harry Bruce, George Bain, and Michelle Lansberg. Carefully examine these columns in terms of the style and structure of a successful newspaper column.

2. Read some selections from *Outrageous Acts and Everyday Rebellions* by Gloria Steinem. Present to your seminar group a report on the most important aspects of Steinem's feminist thinking. Include your own evaluation of her thinking.

3. Write a review of a film by Woody Allen. In your review comment upon Allen's cinematic use of parody, incongruity, and exaggeration.

4. Examine several issues of *Ms. Magazine* in terms of its purpose, audience, policies, and advertising. Write a review of this publication in light of your investigation.

WRITING TO DESCRIBE

Description is the art of creating pictures in words:
"...the thin black branches of poplar and chokecherry now meringued with frost..."
"...the team of giant black horses would cannon forth, pulling the fire wagon like some scarlet chariot of the Goths..."

Through her attention to fine detail, Margaret Laurence builds a composite picture of the town of her childhood. She wants her readers to see the place "where the world began" as she sees it now, a microcosm of the entire country.

Edward O. Wilson is fascinated by snakes: "...a water moccasin... one of the poisonous pit vipers, more than five feet long with a body as thick as my arm and a head the size of a fist." This description clearly indicates the tension that can exist between the perceiver and the object perceived.

Lewis Thomas internalizes the tension between the perceiver and the perceived. This process of internalization is revealed in the diction he employs to describe the behaviour of termites. "...they organize in platoons and begin stacking up pellets to precisely the right height, then turning the arches to connect the columns, constructing the cathedral and its chambers in which the colony will live out its life for the decades ahead, air-conditioned and humidity-controlled, following the chemical blueprint coded in their genes, flawlessly, stone-blind." Here the writer uses metaphors of human behaviour to interpret and describe the actions of termites.

In her portrait of former Canadian Senator Eugene Forsey, Charlotte Gray uses energetic diction: "...Forsey swings his chair around to face his battleship-grey Underwood manual, briskly inserts a clean sheet of erasable bond paper and, his index fingers jabbing away, bashes out a well-argued, witty missive..."

Ray Guy describes a wall of firewood stacked for Christmas with the bristling rhythm of natural imagery: "Some junks of dry and weathered rampikes but most of sappy spruce and balsam fir with turpentine bladders and green twigs sticking off."

Although each of these essayists has a different purpose, all have in common a compelling urgency to share an observation with the reader, not by telling but by showing.

Where the World Began

Margaret Laurence

- Define "microcosm."
- In what ways is your community a microcosm?
- How has your birthplace influenced your development—your personality, values, beliefs?

A strange place it was, that place where the world began. A place of incredible happenings, splendours and revelations, despairs like multitudinous pits of isolated hells. A place of shadow-spookiness, inhabited by the unknowable dead. A place of jubilation and of mourning, horrible and beautiful.

It was, in fact, a small prairie town.

Because that settlement and that land were my first and for many years my only real knowledge of this planet, in some profound way they remain my world, my way of viewing. My eyes were formed there. Towns like ours, set in a sea of land, have been described thousands of times as dull, bleak, flat, uninteresting. I have had it said to me that the railway trip across Canada is spectacular, except for the prairies, when it would be desirable to go to sleep for several days, until the ordeal is over. I am always unable to argue this point effectively. All I can say is—well, you really have to live there to know that country. The town of my childhood could be called bizarre, agonizingly repressive or cruel at times, and the land in which it grew could be called harsh in the violence of its seasonal changes. But never merely flat or uninteresting. Never dull.

In winter, we used to hitch rides on the back of the milk sleigh, our moccasins squeaking and slithering on the hard rutted snow of the roads, our hands in ice-bubbled mitts hanging onto the box edge of the sleigh for dear life, while Bert grinned at us through his great frosted moustache and shouted the horse into speed, daring us to stay put. Those mornings, rising, there would be the perpetual fascination of the frost feathers on windows, the ferns and flowers and eerie faces traced there during the night by unseen artists of the wind. Evenings, coming back from skating, the sky would be black but not dark, for you could see a cold glitter of stars from one side of the earth's rim to the other. And then the sometime astonishment when you saw the Northern Lights flaring across the sky, like the scrawled signature of God. After a blizzard, when the snowploughs hadn't yet got through, school would be closed for the day, the assumption being that the town's young could not possibly flounder through five feet of snow in the pursuit of education. We would then gaily don snowshoes and flounder for miles out into the white dazzling deserts, in pursuit of a different kind of knowing. If you came back too close to night, through the woods at the foot of the town hill, the thin black branches of poplar and chokecherry now meringued with frost, sometimes you heard coyotes. Or maybe the banshee wolf-voices were really only inside your head.

Summers were scorching, and when no rain came and the wheat became bleached and dried before it headed, the faces of farmers and townsfolk would not smile much, and you took for granted, because it never seemed to have been any different, the frequent knocking at the back door and the young men standing there, mumbling or thrusting defiantly their requests for a drink of water and a sandwich if you could spare it. They were riding the freights, and you never knew where they had come from, or where they might end up, if anywhere. The Drought and Depression were like evil deities which had been there always. You understood and did not understand.

Yet the outside world had its continuing marvels. The poplar bluffs and the small river were filled and surrounded with a zillion different grasses, stones, and weed flowers. The meadowlarks sang undaunted from the twanging telephone wires along the gravel highway. Once we found an old flat-bottomed scow, and launched her, poling along the shallow brown waters, mending her with wodges of hastily chewed Spearmint, grounding her among the tangles of yellow marsh marigolds that grew succulently along the banks of the shrunken river, while the sun made our skins smell dusty-warm.

My best friend lived in an apartment above some stores on Main Street (its real name was Mountain Avenue, goodness knows why), an elegant apartment with royal-blue velvet curtains. The back roof, scarcely sloping at all, was corrugated tin, of a furnace-like warmth on a July afternoon, and we would sit there drinking lemonade and looking across the back lane at the Fire Hall. Sometimes our vigil would be rewarded. Oh joy! Somebody's house burning down! We had an almost-perfect callousness in some ways. Then the wooden tower's bronze bell would clonk and toll like a thousand speeded funerals in a time of plague, and in a few minutes the team of giant black horses would cannon forth, pulling the fire wagon like some scarlet chariot of the Goths, while the firemen clung with one hand, adjusting their helmets as they went.

The oddities of the place were endless. An elderly lady used to serve, as her afternoon tea offering to other ladies, soda biscuits spread with peanut butter and topped with a whole marshmallow. Some considered this slightly eccentric, when compared with chopped egg sandwiches, and admittedly talked about her behind her back, but no one ever refused these delicacies or indicated to her that they thought she had slipped a cog. Another lady dyed her hair a bright and cheery orange, by strangers often mistaken at twenty paces for a feather hat. My own beloved stepmother wore a silver fox neckpiece, a whole pelt, *with the embalmed (?) head still on*. My Ontario Irish grandfather said, "sparrow grass," a more interesting term than asparagus. The town dump was known as "the nuisance grounds," a phrase fraught with weird connotations, as though the effluvia of our lives was beneath contempt but at the same time was subtly threatening to the determined and sometimes hysterical propriety of our ways.

Some oddities were, as idiom had it, "funny ha ha"; others were "funny peculiar." Some were not so very funny at all. An old man lived, deranged, in a shack in the valley. Perhaps he wasn't even all that old, but to us he seemed a wild Methuselah figure, shambling among the underbrush and the tall couchgrass, muttering indecipherable curses or blessings, a prophet who had forgotten his prophesies. Everyone in town knew him, but no one knew him. He lived among us as though only occasionally and momentarily visible. The kids called him Andy Gump, and feared him. Some sought to prove their bravery by tormenting him. They were the mediaeval bear baiters, and he the lumbering bewildered bear, half blind, only rarely turning to snarl. Everything is to be found in a town like mine. Belsen, writ small but with the same ink.

All of us cast stones in one shape or another. In grade school, among the vulnerable and violet girls we were, the feared and despised were those few older girls from what was charmingly termed "the wrong side of the tracks." Tough in talk and tougher in muscle, they were said to be whores already. And may have been, that being about the only profession readily available to them.

The dead lived in that place, too. Not only the grandparents who had, in local parlance, "passed on" and who gloomed, bearded or bonneted, from the sepia photographs in old albums, but also the uncles, forever eighteen or nineteen, whose names were carved on the granite family stones in the cemetery, but whose bones lay in France. My own young mother lay in that graveyard, beside other dead of our kin, and when I was ten, my father, too, only forty, left the living town for the dead dwelling on the hill.

When I was eighteen, I couldn't wait to get out of that town, away from the prairies. I did not know then that I would carry the land and town all my life within my skull, that they would form the mainspring and source of the writing I was to do; wherever and however far away I might live.

This was my territory in the time of my youth, and in a sense my life since then has been an attempt to look at it, to come to terms with it. Stultifying to the mind it certainly could be, and sometimes was, but not to the imagination. It was many things, but it was never dull.

The same, I now see, could be said for Canada in general. Why on earth did generations of Canadians pretend to believe this country dull? We knew perfectly well it wasn't. Yet for so long we did not proclaim what we knew. If our upsurge of so-called nationalism seems odd or irrelevant to outsiders, and even to some of own people (*what's all the fuss about?*), they might try to understand that for many years we valued ourselves insufficiently, living as we did under the huge shadows of those two dominating figures, Uncle Sam and Britannia. We have only just begun to value ourselves, our land, our abilities. We have only just begun to recognize our legends and to give shape to our myths.

There are, God knows, enough aspects to deplore about this country. When I see the killing of our lakes and rivers with industrial wastes, I feel rage and despair. When I see our industries and natural resources increasingly taken over by America, I feel an overwhelming discouragement, especially as I cannot simply say "damn Yankees." It should never be forgotten that it is we ourselves who have sold such a large amount of our birthright for a mess of plastic Progress. When I saw the War Measures Act being invoked in 1970, I lost forever the vestigial remains of the naive wish-belief that repression could not happen here, or would not. And yet, of course, I had known all along in the deepest and often hidden caves of the heart that anything can happen anywhere, for the seeds of both man's freedom and his captivity are found everywhere, even in the microcosm of a prairie town. But in raging against our injustices, our stupidities, I do so *as family*, as I did, and still do in writing, about those aspects of my town which I hated and which are always in some ways aspects of myself.

The land still draws me more than other lands. I have lived in Africa and in England, but splendid as both can be, they do not have the power to move in the same way as, for example, that part of southern Ontario where I spent four months last summer in a cedar cabin beside a river. "Scratch a Canadian, and you find a phony pioneer," I used to say to myself in warning. But all the same it is true, I think, that we are not yet totally alienated from physical earth, and let us only pray we do not become so. I once thought that my lifelong fear and mistrust of cities made me a kind of old-fashioned freak; now I see it differently.

The cabin has a long window across its front western wall, and sitting at the oak table there in the mornings, I used to look out at the river and at the tall trees beyond, green-gold in the early light. The river was bronze; the sun caught it strangely, reflecting upon its surface the near-shore sand ripples underneath. Suddenly, the crescenting of a fish, gone before the eye could clearly give image to it. The old man next door said these leaping fish were carp. Himself, he preferred muskie, for he was a real fisherman and the muskie gave him a fight. The wind most often blew from the south, and the river flowed toward the south, so when the water was wind-riffled, and the current was strong, the river seemed to be flowing both ways. I liked this, and interpreted it as an omen, a natural symbol.

A few years ago, when I was back in Winnipeg, I gave a talk at my old college. It was open to the public, and afterward a very old man came up to me and asked me if my maiden name had been Wemyss. I said yes, thinking he might have known my father or my grandfather. But no. "When I was a young lad," he said, "I once worked for your great-grandfather, Robert Wemyss, when he had the sheep ranch at Rae-burn." I think that was a moment when I realized all over again something of great importance to me. My long-ago families came from Scotland and Ireland, but in a sense that no longer mattered so much. My true roots were here.

I am not very patriotic, in the usual meaning of that word. I cannot say "My country right or wrong" in any political, social or literary context. But one thing is inalterable, for better or worse, for life.

This is where my world began. A world which includes the ancestors—both my own and other people's ancestors who become mine. A world which formed me, and continues to do so, even while I fought it in some of its aspects, and continue to do so. A world which gave me my own lifework to do, because it was here that I learned the sight of my own particular eyes.

Thought

1. Evaluate Margaret Laurence's attempt to show the following:
   a) "Everything is to be found in a town like [hers]"
   b) "Stultifying to the mind it certainly could be, and sometimes was, but not to the imagination."
2. Laurence's attention to the particulars of her town is consistent with her assertion, "My eyes were formed there." Give specific details from the essay which support this statement.

Style and Structure

3. How is Laurence's opening sentence an effective beginning for a descriptive essay?
4. Divide the essay into its various units according to each shift in focus. Explain why the author arranges the units in this manner.
5. Using several examples, demonstrate how Laurence's diction evokes a unique and colourful place.

Response and Extension

6. Debate one of the following statements:
   a) "Why on earth did generations of Canadians pretend to believe this country dull? We knew perfectly well it wasn't."
   b) "Scratch a Canadian, and you find a phony pioneer."
7. Write a descriptive essay which evokes the place of your childhood. Focus on a time from your childhood when you felt your neighbourhood or town was the whole world. Describe that world using precise details.

Snakes and Psyche

Edward O. Wilson

- How do you react when you see a snake? Why?
- Discuss the significance of snakes in folklore and mythology.

I grew up in the panhandle of northern Florida and the adjacent counties of Alabama, in circumstances that eventually turned me into a field biologist. Like most boys in that part of the country set loose to roam the woods, I enjoyed hunting and fishing and made no clear distinction between these activities and life at large. But I also cherished natural history for its own sake and decided very early to become a biologist. I had a secret ambition to find a real serpent, a snake so fabulously large or otherwise different that it would exceed the bounds of imagination.

Certain peculiarities in the environment encouraged this adolescent fantasy. That part of the country had been covered, four generations back, by a wilderness as formidable in some respects as the Amazon. The Gulf Coast has a greater variety and a denser population of snakes than almost any other place in the world, and they are frequently seen.

Of course limits to the abundance and diversity exist. Because snakes feed on frogs, mice, fish, and other animals of similar size, they are necessarily scarcer than their prey. You can't just go out on a stroll and point to one snake after another. But I can testify from personal experience that on any given day you are ten times more likely to meet a snake in Florida than in Brazil or New Guinea.

I found my serpent on a still July morning in a swamp, while working toward higher ground along the course of a weed-choked stream. Without warning, a very large snake crashed away under my feet and plunged into the water. Its movement startled me even more than it would have in other circumstances, because I had grown accustomed through the day to modestly proportioned frogs and turtles silently tensed on mudbanks and logs. This snake was more nearly my size, as well as violent and noisy—a colleague, so to speak. It sped with wide body undulations to the center of the shallow watercourse and came to rest on a sandy riffle. It was not quite the monster I had envisioned but nevertheless unusual, a water moccasin (*Agkistrodon piscivorus*), one of the poisonous pit vipers, more than five feet long with a body as thick as my arm and a head the size of a fist. It was the largest snake I had ever seen in the wild. I later calculated it to be just under the published size record for the species. The snake now lay quietly in the shallow, clear water completely open to view, its body stretched along the fringing weeds, its head pointed back at an oblique angle to watch my approach. Moccasins are like that. They don't always keep going until they are out of sight, in the manner of ordinary water snakes. Although no emotion can be read in the frozen half-smile and staring yellow cat's eyes, their reactions and posture make them seem insolent, as if they see their power reflected in the caution of human beings and other sizable enemies.

I moved through the snake handler's routine: pressed the snake stick across the body in back of the head, rolled it forward to pin the head securely, brought one hand around to grasp the neck just behind the swelling masseteric muscles, dropped the stick to seize the body midway back with the other hand, and lifted the entire animal clear of the water. The technique almost always works. The moccasin, however, reacted in a way that took me by surprise and put my life in immediate danger. Throwing its heavy body into convulsions, it twisted its head and neck slightly forward through my gripped fingers, stretched its mouth wide open to unfold the inch-long fangs and expose the dead-white inner lining in the intimidating cottonmouth display. A fetid musk from its anal glands filled the air. At that moment the morning heat became more noticeable, the episode turned manifestly frivolous, and I wondered why I should be in that place alone. Who would find me? The snake began to turn its head far enough to clamp its jaws on my hand. I was not very strong for my age, and I was losing control. Without thinking I heaved the giant into the bush, and it thrashed frantically away, this time until it was out of sight and we were rid of each other.

I sat down and let the adrenaline race my heart and bring tremors to my hand. How could I have been so stupid? What is there in snakes anyway that makes them so repellent and fascinating? The answer in retrospect is deceptively simple: their ability to remain hidden, the power in their sinuous limbless bodies, and the threat from venom injected hypodermically through sharp, hollow teeth. It pays in elementary survival to be interested in snakes and to respond emotionally to their generalized image, to go beyond ordinary caution and fear. The rule built into the brain in the form of a learning bias is: Become alert quickly to any object with the serpentine gestalt. *Overlearn* this particular response in order to keep safe.

Other primates have evolved similar rules. When guenons and vervets, the common monkeys of the African forest, see a python, cobra, or puff adder, they emit a distinctive chuttering call that rouses other members in the group. The monkeys in effect broadcast a dangerous-snake alert, which serves to protect the entire group and not solely the individual who encountered the danger. The most remarkable fact is that the serpent alarm is evoked most strongly by the kinds of snakes that can harm them.

The idea that snake aversion on the part of man's relatives can be an inborn trait is supported by other studies on rhesus macaques, the large brown monkeys of India and surrounding Asian countries. When adults see a snake of any kind, they react with the generalized fear response of their species. They variously back off and stare (or turn away), crouch, shield their faces, bark, screech, and twist their faces into the fear grimace, in which the lips are retracted, the teeth are bared, and the ears are flattened against the head. Monkeys raised in the laboratory without previous exposure to snakes show the same response—although in weaker form—as those brought in from the wild. During control experiments designed to test the specificity of the response, the rhesus monkeys failed to react to other, nonsinuous objects placed in their cages.

Grant for the moment that snake aversion does have a hereditary basis in at least some kinds of nonhuman primates. The possibility that immediately follows is that the trait evolved by natural selection. In other words, individuals who respond leave more offspring than those who do not, and as a result the propensity to learn fear quickly spreads through the population—or, if it was already present, is maintained there at a high level.

How can biologists test such a proposition about the origin of behavior? They search for species historically free of forces in the environment believed to favor the evolutionary change, to see if in fact the organisms do *not* process the trait. The lemurs, primitive relatives of the monkeys, offer such an inverted opportunity. They are indigenous inhabitants of Madagascar, where no large or poisonous snakes exist to threaten them. Sure enough, lemurs in captivity, when presented with snakes, fail to display anything resembling the automatic fear responses of the African and Asian monkeys. Is this adequate proof? In the chaste idiom of scientific discourse, we are permitted to conclude only that the evidence is consistent with the proposal. Neither this nor any comparable hypothesis can be settled by a single case.

Another line of evidence comes from studies of the chimpanzee, a species thought to have shared a common ancestor with prehumans as recently as 5 million years ago. Chimps raised in the laboratory become apprehensive in the presence of snakes, even if they have had no previous experience. They back off to a safe distance and follow the intruder with a fixed stare while alerting companions with the *Wah!* warning call. More important, the response becomes gradually more marked during adolescence.

This last quality is especially interesting because human beings pass through approximately the same developmental sequence. Children under five years of age feel no special anxiety over snakes, but later they grow increasingly wary. Just one or two mildly bad experiences, such as a garter snake seen writhing away in the grass, a playmate thrusting a rubber model at them, or a counselor telling scary stories at the campfire, can make children deeply and permanently fearful. Other common fears, notably of the dark, strangers, and loud noises, start to wane after seven years of age. In contrast, the tendency to avoid snakes grows stronger with time. It is possible to turn the mind in the opposite direction, to learn to handle snakes without apprehension or even to like them in some special way, as I did. But the adaptation takes a special effort and is usually a little forced and self-conscious. The special sensitivity will just as likely lead to full-blown ophidiophobia, the pathological extreme in which the mere appearance of a snake brings on a feeling of panic, cold sweat, and waves of nausea. I have witnessed these events.

At a campsite in Alabama, on a Sunday afternoon, a four-foot-long black racer glided out from the woods, across the clearing, and headed for the high grass along a nearby stream. Children shouted and pointed. A middle-aged woman screamed and collapsed to the ground sobbing. Her husband dashed to his pickup truck to get a shotgun. But black racers are among the fastest snakes in the world and this one made it safely to cover. The onlookers probably did not know that the species is harmless to any creature larger than a cotton rat.

Halfway around the world, at the village of Ebabaang, in New Guinea, I heard shouting and saw people running down a path. When I caught up with them they had formed a circle around a small brown snake that was slithering leisurely across the front yard of a house. I pinned the snake and carried it off to be preserved in alcohol for the museum collections at Harvard. This seeming act of daring earned either the admiration or the suspicion of my hosts—I couldn't be sure which. The next day children followed me around as I gathered insects in the nearby forest. One brought me an immense, orb-weaving spider gripped in his fingers, its hairy legs waving and the evil-looking black fangs working up and down. I felt panicky and sick. It so happens that I suffer from mild arachnophobia. To each his own.

Why should serpents have such a strong influence during mental development? The direct and simple answer is that throughout history a few kinds have been a major cause of sickness and death. Every continent except Antarctica has poisonous snakes. Over large stretches of Asia and Africa the known death rate from snake bite is five persons per 100,000 each year, or higher. The local record is held by a province in Burma, with 36.8 deaths per 100,000 a year. The number of people bitten in such improbable places as Switzerland and Finland is still high enough, running into the hundreds annually, to keep outdoorsmen on a sort of yellow alert.

For hundreds of thousands of years, time enough for the appropriate genetic changes to have occurred in the brain, poisonous snakes have been a significant source of injury and death to human beings. We need not turn to Freudian theory in order to explain our special relationship to snakes. The serpent did not originate as the vehicle of dreams and symbols. The relation appears to be precisely the other way around. Humanity's concrete experience with poisonous snakes gave rise to the Freudian phenomena after it was assimilated by genetic evolution into the brain's structure. The mind has to create symbols and fantasies from something. It leans toward the most powerful preexistent images or at least follows the learning rules that create the images, including that of the serpent. For most of this century, perhaps overly enchanted by psychoanalysis, we have confused the dream with the reality and its psychic effect with the ultimate cause rooted in nature.

Thought

1. Why does Wilson find snakes both "repellent and fascinating"? Find details in the essay which demonstrate his conflicting feelings.
2. What evidence does Wilson present to prove that fear of snakes is a biological, not a psychological phenomenon?

Style and Structure

3. With reference to several examples show that Wilson uses description to support his thesis.
4. What does Wilson achieve through the anecdote about the water moccasin?

Response and Extension

5. Write an essay which discusses one of your phobias, real or fictitious. Include a description of the symptoms, the effects the phobia has upon your life, and the advice you have received on how to deal with it.

Seven Wonders

Lewis Thomas

- List the seven wonders of the ancient world. What do they have in common?
- List seven wonders of the last decade. What do they have in common?
- List the things you wonder about most.

A while ago I received a letter from a magazine editor inviting me to join six other people at dinner to make a list of the Seven Wonders of the Modern World, to replace the seven old, out-of-date Wonders. I replied that I couldn't manage it, not on short order anyway, but still the question keeps hanging around in the lobby of my mind. I had to look up the old biodegradable Wonders, the Hanging Gardens of Babylon and all the rest, and then I had to look up that word "wonder" to make sure I understood what it meant. It occurred to me that if the magazine could get any seven people to agree on a list of any such seven things you'd have the modern Seven Wonders right there at the dinner table.

Wonder is a word to wonder about. It contains a mixture of messages: something marvelous and miraculous, surprising, raising unanswerable questions about itself, making the observer wonder, even raising skeptical questions like, "I *wonder* about that." Miraculous and marvelous are clues; both words come from an ancient Indo-European root meaning simply to smile or to laugh. Anything wonderful is something to smile in the presence of, in admiration (which, by the way, comes from the same root, along with, of all telling words, "mirror").

I decided to try making a list, not for the magazine's dinner party but for this occasion: seven things I wonder about the most.

I shall hold the first for the last, and move along.

My Number Two Wonder is a bacterial species never seen on the face of the earth until 1982, creatures never dreamed of before, living violation of what we used to regard as the laws of nature, things literally straight out of Hell. Or anyway what we used to think of as Hell, the hot unlivable interior of the earth. Such regions have recently come into scientific view from the research submarines designed to descend twenty-five hundred meters or more to the edge of deep holes in the sea bottom, where open vents spew superheated seawater in plumes from chimneys in the earth's crust, known to oceanographic scientists as "black smokers." This is not just hot water, or steam, or even steam under pressure as exists in a laboratory autoclave (which we have relied upon for decades as the surest way to destroy all microbial life). This is extremely hot water under extremely high pressure, with temperatures in excess of 300 degrees centigrade. At such heat, the existence of life as we know it would be simply inconceivable. Proteins and DNA would fall apart, enzymes would melt away, anything alive would die instantaneously. We have long since ruled out the possibility of life on Venus because of that planet's comparable temperature; we have ruled out the possibility of life in the earliest years of this planet, four billion or so years ago, on the same ground.

B.J.A. Baross and J.W. Deming have recently discovered the presence of thriving colonies of bacteria in water fished directly from these deep-sea vents. Moreover, when brought to the surface, encased in titanium syringes and sealed in pressurized chambers heated to 250 degrees centigrade, the bacteria not only survive but reproduce themselves enthusiastically. They can be killed only by chilling them down in boiling water.

And yet they look just like ordinary bacteria. Under the electron microscope they have the same essential structure—cell walls, ribosomes, and all. If they were, as is now being suggested, the original archebacteria, ancestors of us all, how did they or their progeny ever learn to cool down? I cannot think of a more wonderful trick.

My Number Three Wonder is *oncideres*, a species of beetle encountered by a pathologist friend of mine who lives in Houston and has a lot of mimosa trees in his backyard. This beetle is not new, but it qualifies as a Modern Wonder because of the exceedingly modern questions raised for evolutionary biologists about the three consecutive things on the mind of the female of the species. Her first thought is for a mimosa tree, which she finds and climbs, ignoring all other kinds of trees in the vicinity. Her second thought is for the laying of eggs, which she does by crawling out on a limb, cutting a longitudinal slit with her mandible and depositing her eggs beneath the slit. Her third and last thought concerns the welfare of her offspring; beetle larvae cannot survive in live wood, so she backs up a foot or so and cuts a neat circular girdle all around the limb, through the bark and down into the cambium. It takes her eight hours to finish this cabinetwork. Then she leaves and where she goes I do not know. The limb dies from the girdling, falls to the ground in the next breeze, the larvae feed and grow into the next generation, and the questions lie there unanswered. How on earth did these three linked thoughts in her mind evolve together in evolution? How could any one of the three become fixed as beetle behavior by itself, without the other two? What are the odds favoring three totally separate bits of behavior—like a particular tree, cutting a slit for eggs, and then girdling the limb—happening together by random chance among a beetle's genes? Does this smart beetle know what she is doing? And how did the mimosa tree enter the picture in its evolution? Left to themselves, unpruned, mimosa trees have a life expectancy of twenty-five to thirty years. Pruned each year, which is what the beetle's girdling labor accomplishes, the tree can flourish for a century. The mimosa-beetle relationship is an elegant example of symbiotic partnership, a phenomenon now recognized as pervasive in nature. It is good for us to have around on our intellectual mantelpiece such creatures as this insect and its friend the tree, for they keep reminding us how little we know about nature.

The Fourth Wonder on my list is an infectious agent known as the scrapie virus, which causes a fatal disease of the brain in sheep, goats, and several laboratory animals. A close cousin of scrapie is the C-J virus, the cause of some cases of senile dementia in human beings. These are called "slow viruses," for the excellent reason that an animal exposed to infection today will not become ill until a year and a half or two years from today. The agent, whatever it is, can propagate itself in abundance from a few infectious units today to more than a billion next year. I use the phrase "whatever it is" advisedly. Nobody has yet been able to find any DNA or RNA in the scrapie or C-J viruses. It may be there, but if so it exists in amounts too small to detect. Meanwhile, there is plenty of protein, leading to a serious proposal that the virus may indeed be *all* protein. But protein, so far as we know, does not replicate itself all by itself, not on this planet anyway. Looked at this way, the scrapie agent seems the strangest thing in all biology and, until someone in some laboratory figures out what it is, a candidate for Modern Wonder.

My Fifth Wonder is the olfactory receptor cell, located in the epithelial tissue high in the nose, sniffing the air for clues to the environment, the fragrance of friends, the smell of leaf smoke, breakfast, nighttime and bedtime, and a rose, even, it is said, the odor of sanctity. The cell that does all these things, firing off urgent messages into the deepest parts of the brain, switching on one strange unaccountable memory after another, is itself a proper brain cell, a certified neuron belonging to the brain but miles away out in the open air, nosing around the world.

How it manages to make sense of what it senses, discriminating between jasmine and anything else non-jasmine with infallibility, is one of the deep secrets of neurobiology. This would be wonder enough, but there is more. This population of brain cells, unlike any other neurons of the vertebrate central nervous system, turns itself over every few weeks; cells wear out, die, and are replaced by brand-new cells rewired to the same deep centers miles back in the brain, sensing and remembering the same wonderful smells. If and when we reach an understanding of these cells and their functions, including the moods and whims under their governance, we will know a lot more about the mind than we do now, a world away.

Sixth on my list is, I hesitate to say, another insect, the termite. This time, though, it is not the single insect that is the Wonder, it is the collectivity. There is nothing at all wonderful about a single, solitary termite, indeed there is really no such creature, functionally speaking, as a lone termite, any more than we can imagine a genuinely solitary human being; no such thing. Two or three termites gathered together on a dish are not much better; they may move about and touch each other nervously, but nothing happens. But keep adding more termites until they reach a critical mass, and then the miracle begins. As though they had suddenly received a piece of extraordinary news, they organize in platoons and begin stacking up pellets to precisely the right height, then turning the arches to connect the columns, constructing the cathedral and its chambers in which the colony will live out its life for the decades ahead, air-conditioned and humidity-controlled, following the chemical blueprint coded in their genes, flawlessly, stone-blind. They are not the dense mass of individual insects they appear to be; they are an organism, a thoughtful, meditative brain on a million legs. All we really know about this new thing is that it does its architecture and engineering by a complex system of chemical signals.

The Seventh Wonder of the modern world is a human child, any child. I used to wonder about childhood and the evolution of our species. It seemed to me unparsimonious to keep expending all that energy on such a long period of vulnerability and defenselessness, with nothing to show for it, in biological terms, beyond the feckless, irresponsible pleasure of childhood. After all, I used to think, it is one sixth of a whole human life span! Why didn't our evolution take care of that, allowing us to jump catlike from our juvenile to our adult (and, as I thought) productive stage of life? I had forgotten about language, the single human trait that marks us out as specifically human, the property that enables our survival as the most compulsively, biologically, obsessively social of all creatures on earth, more interdependent and interconnected even than the famous social insects. I had forgotten that, and forgotten that children *do* that in childhood. Language is what childhood is for.

There is another related but different creature, nothing like so wonderful as a human child, nothing like so hopeful, something to worry about all day and all night. It is *us*, aggregated together in our collective, critical masses. So far, we have learned how to be useful to each other only when we collect in small groups—families, circles of friends, once in a while (although still rarely) committees. The drive to be useful is encoded in our genes. But when we gather in very large numbers, as in the modern nation-state, we seem capable of levels of folly and self-destruction to be found nowhere else in all of Nature.

As a species, taking all in all, we are still too young, too juvenile, to be trusted. We have spread across the face of the earth in just a few thousand years, no time at all as evolution clocks time, covering all livable parts of the planet, endangering other forms of life, and now threatening ourselves. As a species, we have everything in the world to learn about living, but we may be running out of time. Provisionally, but only provisionally, we are a Wonder.

And now the first on my list, the one I put off at the beginning of making a list, the first of all Wonders of the modern world. To name this one, you have to redefine the world as it has indeed been redefined in this most scientific of all centuries. We named the place we live in the *world* long ago, from the Indo-European root *wiros*, which meant man. We now live in the whole universe, that stupefying piece of expanding geometry. Our suburbs are the local solar system, into which, sooner or later, we will spread life, and then, likely, beyond into the galaxy. Of all celestial bodies within reach or view, as far as we can see, out to the edge, the most wonderful and marvelous and mysterious is turning out to be our own planet earth. There is nothing to match it anywhere, not yet anyway.

It is a living system, an immense organism, still developing, regulating itself, making its own oxygen, maintaining its own temperature, keeping all its infinite living parts connected and interdependent, including us. It is the strangest of all places, and there is everything in the world to learn about it. It can keep us awake and jubilant with questions for millennia ahead, if we can learn not to meddle and not to destroy. Our great hope is in being such a young species, thinking in language only a short while, still learning, still growing up.

We are not like the social insects. They have only the one way of doing things and they will do it forever, coded for that way. We are coded differently, not just for binary choices, *go* or *no-go*. We can go four ways at once, depending on how the air feels: *go, no-go*, but also *maybe*, plus *what the hell let's give it a try.* We are in for one surprise after another if we keep at it and keep alive. We can build structures for human society never seen before, thoughts never thought before, music never heard before.

Provided we do not kill ourselves off, and provided we can connect ourselves by the affection and respect for which I believe our genes are also coded, there is no end to what we might do on or off this planet.

At this early stage in our evolution, now through our infancy and into our childhood and then, with luck, our growing up, what our species needs most of all, right now, is simply a future.

Thought

1. List Thomas' seven wonders. What criteria have determined his choices?
2. How do these "wonders" differ from the seven wonders of the ancient world? How do they differ from your choices of the seven wonders of the last decade?
3. Summarize Thomas' thoughts on language.

Style and Structure

4. What is the purpose of the second paragraph?
5. Which of Thomas' seven wonders do you find most interesting? How has Thomas made its description interesting to you?
6. For what reasons does the author discuss his first "wonder" last?
7. Explain the relationship between the three concluding paragraphs and the rest of the essay.

Response and Extension

8. a) List your own seven wonders.
   b) Write a description of one of these wonders based on your own criteria.
9. Write a journal entry about something wonderful that has happened to you. What made it "wonderful"?

Letterman

Charlotte Gray

- Have you ever written a letter to the editor of a newspaper? Why? Why not?
- What do you think is the intended effect of letters to the editor?
- What do you think is the actual effect?
- On what basis do you think letters to the editor are published?

"I seldom set out to write a letter," explains Eugene Forsey, enthusiastically bouncing backwards and forwards in his chair. "But then I pick up the newspaper and see some outrageously foolish, wrong-headed, stupid, or ignorant statement and I take fire." At the age of eighty-two ex-Senator Eugene Forsey is the Canadian champion writer of letters to the editor. His favourite outlet is *The Globe and Mail*, but over the last sixty years most major Canadian dailies have carried his barbs. Forsey doesn't always keep copies of his letters, and has no idea how many he has written over his lifetime. He is compelled by the urge to get things right. As the flame of indignation leaps, Forsey swings his chair around to face his battleship-grey Underwood manual, briskly inserts a clean sheet of erasable bond paper and, his two index fingers jabbing away, bashes out a well-argued, witty missive on anything from dogs to doctors. No subject is too picayune or obscure. When such a letter arrives on the desk of Jack Kapica, who edits the *Globe* letters page, Kapica recognizes it as a Forsey before he's even read the contents, double-spaced to allow for editing changes. "The man is astonishing," says Kapica. "Some days I'll receive three or four letters, on completely different subjects but all accurate and succinct."

Forsey's compulsion originates partly in his prodigious memory. And in his life there has been much to remember. His grandfather, W.C.

Bowles, was a towering figure in Ottawa: a frock-coated Victorian who retired in 1915 as a chief clerk of the House of Commons. His mother, librarian to the Geological Survey of Canada, imparted to her only child a well-developed sense of history. One day she introduced him to a French officer who had arrived in Ottawa as part of an Anglo-French war mission. "When you grow up," she said, "I want you to be able to say that you met the celebrated Captain Dreyfus." But there is more to Forsey's passion for accuracy than total recall. He represents a unique stand in the Canadian psyche—a mix of his grandfather's high-principled Ontario Methodism with the high-spirited vigour of his father's native Newfoundland. "I react very strongly when people's toes are trodden on," Forsey explains in a breathless lilt.

From McGill, Forsey won a Rhodes scholarship to Oxford. Three years there reinforced his ardent interest in socialism and his tendency to boil with rage at social injustice. "In England infringement of the civil liberties of even an unsavoury person arouses public indignation. When I returned to Canada in 1929, the inclination to take things lying down irked me extraordinarily. That started me writing to newspapers, in defence of the unemployed and others who were having a thin time of it."

The Montreal *Gazette* was an early recipient. Forsey was then a lecturer in political science at McGill. His main antagonist was P.C. Armstrong, economic adviser to the president of Canadian Pacific Railways: "a hard-shell, eighteenth-century free enterpriser who roused my ire over and over again." They conducted long running literary fisticuffs. In 1941 Forsey left McGill to become director of research at the Canadian Congress of Labour in Ottawa. A couple of years later he was engaged in a three-month exchange with the most powerful newspaper editor of the day, J.W. Dafoe of the *Winnipeg Free Press*.

Throughout Forsey's lifetime each crisis in Canadian history has been signposted by at least one of his letters to the editor. During the 1956 pipeline debate, in a letter published in the Ottawa *Journal*, he took the Speaker to task for misuse of the closure rule. "My letter was raised in the House as a matter of privilege and there was a frightful storm," he chuckles. The furore helped precipitate the events of Black Friday that brought down the Liberal government of Louis St. Laurent.

A year after Forsey's retirement from the CLC in 1969, Prime Minister Trudeau offered the old warrior a seat in the Senate. It was the perfect launching pad for a constitutional crusader. In 1977 a *Globe* article suggesting that Canada should be broken up into ten separate tariff and monetary units, with a central government as referee, prompted Forsey to ask the editor, "How many would leap to their feet to sing:

O Canada! Beloved Referee
Of customs dues and banking policy!"

Forsey suggested a single flag for the new units: "10 jackasses eating their leaves off a single maple tree."

After eight years as a senator, Forsey left the red chamber gracefully when he reached seventy-five. But last year he was installed in a little office in the Senate. His Underwood is busier than ever. After American bombs dropped on Tripoli, a *Globe* editorialist applauded the "moral rightness" of the U.S. retaliation for terrorism, and referred to "Sheriff Ronald Reagan." Forsey took fire. "What international authority made him sheriff, or gave him any authority to take this action?" Two days later he was back, taking issue with a headline: "Please tell your headline writer that 'rankle' is an intransitive verb. Something rankles *in* something or *in* somebody."

In Eugene Forsey, sloppiness of research, analysis, or writing rankles. "If he didn't exist," says Kapica, "we'd have to invent him. On constitutional issues he's the public conscience of Canada."

Thought

1. Why did Forsey begin to write letters to the editor?
2. Show that Charlotte Gray proves that for Forsey "no subject is too picayune or obscure" to warrant a letter to the editor.
3. What aspects of Forsey's background qualify him to be "the public conscience of Canada"?

Style and Structure

4. Examine Forsey's statements quoted by Charlotte Gray. Explain how these statements contribute to a description of the man.
5. What image of Forsey is created by Gray's diction in the first paragraph?
6. What principle has Gray used to organize the body of the descriptive essay?
7. Why do you think Gray has omitted specific physical details in her portrait of Eugene Forsey?

RESPONSE AND EXTENSION

8. Read several letters to the editor from major Canadian daily newspapers. In your group, develop a working model of an effective letter to the editor.

9. Read several editorials and compose a letter to the editor in response to one of them.

Christmas in the Bay

Ray Guy

- Describe the aspects of Christmas preparation that you most anticipate every year.
- What changes in your family's behaviour do you notice just before Christmas?

In the last week of Advent the house smelled like a forest.

Behind the kitchen stove, stacked as neatly as books on library shelves, was a wall of firewood. Some junks of dry and weathered rampikes but most of sappy spruce and balsam fir with turpentine bladders and green twigs sticking off.

The heat from the stove brought out the smell. Out in the porch there were firewood reinforcements. The woodbox was full; it was piled high and at both ends.

In all, there was enough firewood in the house and ready to do, along with a few scuttles of coal, for twelve days and twelve nights.

Some say the artificial Christmas trees are disappointing because there's no smell on them. In the mid-nineteen-forties, Christmas trees were still uncommon out around the bay but you wouldn't have noticed the smell of one anyway for the aroma off the twelve-day's supply of firewood.

The kitchen stove was the only source of heat in the house. It was allowed to die out at night and was relit each morning with splits and shavings.

Indeed, people passed every night of the winter in uninsulated houses with no fire, no storm windows. If it was ten degrees out of doors, by morning it could be ten degrees in the bedrooms.

They kept warm on mattresses stuffed with the feathers and down of chickens and wild birds, covered over with quilts and comforters stuffed with wool.

Now we have a fuel crisis and great countries are plunged into distress because thermostats have to be turned down to sixty-eight degrees.

Christmas lasted a whole twelve days then. It was the most remarkable celebration of the year. Even weddings did not come close to it.

Everything possible was done to see that work was cut to a bare minimum during these twelve days. Enough firewood was in and the water-barrels in the porch brimmed full of water from the well.

All of the laundry, baking, scrubbing, butchering, brewing, polishing, mending, patching and cleaning had been done until seven days into the New Year.

There was little work to be done in Christmas except to shovel the drifts from the door in the morning and feed the hens, sheep, horse and cow in the evening.

Christmas now is a glorified weekend. People then apparently determined to give themselves the whole twelve days because they knew they needed it. It was not coincidence that a hard-working people gave themselves the longest break of the year at such a time.

It is the darkest time of year; the long, hard winter stretches ahead. So why not shatter the darkness and gloom with a glorious bash that was the highlight of the year in those times and would be impossible to achieve in today's society.

Considering the circumstances, Christmas then was a heroically defiant thing, a blaze of light hurled by puny men against the longest night; a brazen riotous celebration to say that in the midst of darkness the Saviour was born and the people would live through the cold, both in body and soul.

It was a most positive and optimistic thing.

During those twelve days people would do things they wouldn't dream of doing during the rest of the year.

For instance, they got drunk. Well, not "drunk" as the word means today, but they had "a drop in." Respectable, stern, sober pillars of the church had to be helped home once or twice through Christmas along the slippery roads by boys holding them up and they beaming happily and misplacing their feet as if they were the very lords of misrule.

But people said, "Oh, well, 'tis Christmas, you know." It was just not done to even recall in July that these stern old greyhairs had danced so wild in the reels on St. Stephen's Day.

The turkey wasn't invented yet but there were rabbits in the bakepot and turrs in the oven. There were fowls stewed tender with onions and stuffing and the carcass of a lamb or pig hanging down in the store over the water where it would keep.

There were ducks and geese and venison and salt water birds. There were herring and potatoes and bread. There was jam yesterday, today and tomorrow. There were candies and brew and brandy from St. Peter's.

And there was rum washed out of rum puncheons and wine in bottles from Madeira. There was lots of church, and the poles with the kerosene lamps on them on both sides of the aisle were wrapped in evergreen boughs and tissue-paper roses.

If there was snow there was lots of coming down hills on all sorts of slides in the nights when the moon was bright as day.

There were all the men and boys playing football with a blown-up pig's bladder covered over and stitched with sail canvas.

There was everything. There was everything for everybody.

And the old ladies said, well, perhaps they would, since it was Christmas, have just a little stain, just a little stain for their stomach's sake and... Oh, my it made them right giddy-headed, ha, ha.

On New Years night the church bell would ring and all the guns fired off just like at a wedding because, I suppose, they were taking another New Year for better for worse, for richer or poorer, in sickness and in health....

And Old Christmas Day was almost as good as Christmas Day except a little smaller and it was said you could go up to the stable at twelve o'clock in the night and hear the beasts talk.

Then that was it for another year and it was a good thing.

Thought

1. a) What aspects of Christmas described by Ray Guy are most consistent with your own experience?
    b) Which aspects are most foreign to your experience? Explain.
2. Why is there no mention of gift giving?

Style and Structure

3. List the richest words and phrases which Guy uses to appeal to each of the senses. Explain why these words and phrases appeal to you.
4. What effect does Guy achieve with his lists of objects and activities?
5. How has Guy made effective use of direct quotations?
6. Is there anything in Guy's description which places it in a specific locale? Explain.

Response and Extension

7. Write a description of your own experience of Christmas or of any other major festival time which is a significant part of your life.

8. Investigate and report upon the significance of a symbol or practice associated with a particular religious festival, e.g., the Menorah, Easter eggs, fasting.

Unit Synthesis

1. Read one of Margaret Laurence's "Manawaka" novels. Write an essay which compares the descriptions of Manawaka with the town described in "Where the World Began."

2. Read "Reply to the U.S. Government" (p.186) by Chief Seattle. Compare and contrast the attitudes of Chief Seattle and Margaret Laurence to the lands of their birth.

3. Read the poems "Snake" by D.H. Lawrence, and "A Narrow Fellow in the Grass" by Emily Dickinson. Compare the psychological attitudes of the observers in these two poems to that of Wilson in "Snakes and Psyche."

4. Read a collection of essays by Lewis Thomas: *Lives of a Cell, The Medusa and The Snail,* or *Late Night Thoughts on Listening to Mahler's Ninth Symphony.* Select several passages of description which appeal to you. Present a seminar on Thomas' skills as an observer.

5. Listen to Dylan Thomas' reading of his "A Child's Christmas In Wales."

6. Read *A Christmas Carol* by Charles Dickens. Select a segment of this work and, as a group, write and record on tape your own dramatization of the segment.

7. Read *The First Cuckoo* edited by Kenneth Gregory, a collection of letters to the editor of *The Times* of London. Present one or two of these letters, written by prominent historical or literary figures, to your group. Comment upon the content of the letter, the writer's style and sense of audience.

WRITING TO DEFINE

To define is to set limits. An essay of definition delineates a subject through a careful examination of its particulars.

"The image of the barbarian represents a force to be feared: power without intelligence, matter without mind, an enemy that must be conquered by culture." This is but one of the many faces which constitute our composite image of the enemy as defined by Sam Keen.

In attempting to define marriage, Katherine Anne Porter finds herself writing not of vows and pledges, commitments and contracts, but instead of love. "Love is a state in which one lives who loves, and whoever loves has given himself away; love then, and not marriage, is belonging."

"Love, like music and painting, resists analysis in words," concedes Robertson Davies. In proceeding to define the pleasures of love however, Davies asserts that "a real, enduring love-affair, in marriage and out of it, is an extremely exclusive club of which the entire membership is two co-equal Perpetual Presidents."

In these essays, the enemy, love and marriage are defined. Keen, Porter and Davies systematically examine their topics to present a clear understanding and to refute myth, rumour and falsehood. They reinterpret conventional notions and provide new information in their definitions. They bring us to a new understanding, thereby urging us to alter our behaviour.

Faces of the Enemy

Sam Keen

- Compile a list of adjectives used to describe an enemy.
- What do these adjectives indicate about our perception of the enemy?
- What are the essential characteristics of an enemy?
- To whom are you "the enemy"? Why?

The world, as always, is debating the issues of war and peace. Conservatives believe safety lies in more arms and increased firepower. Liberals place their trust in disarmament and a nuclear freeze. I suggest we will be saved by neither fire nor ice, that the solutions being offered by the political right and left miss the mark. Our problem lies not in our technology, but in our minds, in our ancient tendency to create our enemies in our own imagination.

Our best hope for avoiding war is to understand the psychology of this enmity, the ways in which our mind works to produce our habits of paranoia, projection, and the making of propaganda. How do we create our enemies and turn the world into a killing ground?

We first need to answer some inevitable objections, raised by the advocates of power politics, who say: "You can't psychologize political conflict. You can't solve the problem of war by studying perception. We don't *create* enemies. There are real aggressors—Hitler, Stalin, Qaddafi."

True: There are always political, economic, and territorial causes of war. Wars come and go; the images we use to dehumanize our enemies remain strangely the same. The unchanging projections of the hostile imagination are continually imposed onto changing historical circumstances. Not that the enemy is innocent of these projections—as popular wisdom has it, paranoids sometimes have *real* enemies. Nevertheless, to understand the hostile imagination we need to temporarily ignore the question of guilt and innocence. Our quest is for an understanding of the unchanging images we place on the enemy.

THE ENEMY AS CREATED BY PARANOIA

Paranoia is not an occasional individual pathology, but rather it is the human condition. History shows us that, with few exceptions, social cohesion within tribes is maintained by paranoia: when we do not have enemies, we invent them. The group identity of a people depends on division between insiders and outsiders, us and them, the tribe and the enemy.

The first meaning of *the enemy* is simply the stranger, the alien. The bond of tribal membership is maintained by projecting hostile and divisive emotions upon the outsider. Paranoia forms the mold from which we create enemies.

In the paranoid imagination, *alien* means the same as *evil*, while the tribe itself is defined as good: a single network of malevolent intent stretches over the rest of the world. "They" are out to get "us." All occurrences prove the basic assumption that an outside power is conspiring against the community.

THE ENEMY AS ENEMY OF GOD

In the language of rhetoric, every war is a crusade, a "just" war, a battle between good and evil. Warfare is a ritual in which the sacred blood of our heroes is sacrificed to destroy the enemies of God.

We like to think that theocracies and holy wars ended with the coming of the Industrial Revolution and the emergence of secular cultures in the West. Yet in World War I the kaiser was pictured as the devil; in World War II both Germany and the U.S. proclaimed *Gott mit uns*, "In God We Trust"; each accused the other of being Christ-killers. Sophisticated politicians may insist that the conflict between the U.S. and the USSR is a matter of pragmatic power politics, but theological dimensions have not disappeared. President Reagan warns us against "the aggressive impulses of an evil empire" and asks us to "pray for the salvation of all those who live in totalitarian darkness, pray they will discover the joy of knowing God."

By picturing the enemy as the enemy of God we convert the guilt associated with murder into pride. A warrior who kills such an enemy strikes a blow for truth and goodness. Remorse isn't necessary. The warrior engaged in righteous battle against the enemies of God may even see himself as a priest, saving his enemy from the grip of evil by killing him.

THE ENEMY AS BARBARIAN

The enemy not only is a demon but is also a destroyer of culture. If he is human at all, he is brutish, dumb, and cruel, lower on the scale of evolution than The People. To the Greeks he was a barbarian. To the Americans he was, most recently, a "gook" or "slant." To the South African he is a black or "colored."

The barbarian theme was used widely in World War II propaganda by all participants. Nazi anti-semitic tracts contrasted the sunny, healthy Aryan with the inferior, dark, and contaminated races—Jews, Gypsies, Eastern Europeans. American soldiers were pictured as Chicago-style gangsters. Blacks were portrayed as quasi-gorillas despoiling the artistic achievements of European civilization. One poster used in Holland warned the Dutch that their supposed "liberators" were a mélange of KKK, jazz-crazed blacks, convicts, hangmen, and mad bombers. In turn, the U.S. frequently pictured the Germans as a Nazi horde of dark monsters on a mindless rampage.

The image of the barbarian represents a force to be feared: power without intelligence, matter without mind, an enemy that must be conquered by culture. The warrior who defeats the barbarian is a culture hero, keeping the dark powers in abeyance.

THE ENEMY AS RAPIST

Associated with the enemy as barbarian is the image of the enemy as rapist, the destroyer of motherhood.

As rapist, the enemy is lust defiling innocence. He is according to Nazi propaganda the Jew who lurks in the shadows waiting to seduce Aryan girls. Or in the propaganda of the Ku Klux Klan he is the black man with an insatiable lust for white women. In American war posters he is the Jap carrying away the naked Occidental woman.

The portrait of the enemy as rapist, destroyer of the madonna, warns us of danger and awakens our pornographic imagination by reminding us of the enticement of rape. The appeal to sexual adventure is a sine qua non in motivating men to go to war: To the warrior belong the spoils, and chief among the spoils are the enemy's women.

THE ENEMY AS BEAST, INSECT, REPTILE

The power of bestial images to degrade is rooted in the neurotic structure of the hostile imagination. Karen Horney has shown that neurosis always involves a movement between glorified and degraded images of the self. In warfare we act out a mass neurosis whereby we glorify ourselves as agents of God and project our feelings of degradation and impotence upon the enemy. We are suprahuman; therefore they must be subhuman. By destroying the bestial and contaminated enemy we can gain immortality, escape evil, transcend decay and death.

THE ENEMY AS DEATH

In the iconography of propaganda, the enemy is the bringer of death. He is Death riding on a bomb, the Grim Reaper cutting down youth in its prime. His face is stripped of flesh, his body a dangling skeleton.

War is an irrational ritual. Generation after generation we sacrifice our substance in a vain effort to kill some essential enemy. Now he wears an American or Soviet face. A moment ago he was a Nazi, a Jew, a Moslem, a Christian, a pagan. But the true face of the enemy, as Saint Paul said, is Death itself. The unconscious power that motivates us to fight for Peace, kill for Life, is the magical assumption that if we can destroy this particular enemy we can defeat Death.

Lying within each of us is the desire for immortality. And because this near-instinctive desire for immortality is balanced by the precariously repressed fear that death might really eradicate all traces of our existence, we will go to any extreme to reassure ourselves. By submitting to the divine ordeal of war, in which we are willing to die or kill the enemy who *is* Death, we affirm our own deathlessness.

THE RELUCTANT KILLERS

It is easy to despair when we look at the human genius for creating enemies in the image of our own disowned vices. When we add our mass paranoia and projection to our constantly progressing weapons technology, it seems we are doomed to destroy ourselves.

But the persistent archetypal images of the enemy may point in a more hopeful direction. We demean our enemies not because we are instinctively sadistic, but because it is difficult for us to kill others whom we recognize as fully human beings. Our natural empathy, our instinct for compassion, is strong: society does what it must to attempt to overcome the moral imperative that forbids us from killing.

Even so, the effort is successful only for a minority. In spite of our best propaganda, few men and women will actually try to kill an enemy. In his book *Men Against Fire*, Brigadier General S.L.A. Marshall presents the results of his study of American soldiers under fire during World War II. He discovered that *in combat* the percentage of men who would fire their rifle at the enemy *even once* did not rise above 25 percent, and the more usual figure was 15 percent. He further discovered that the fear of killing was every bit as strong as the fear of dying.

If it is difficult to mold men into killers, we may still hope to transform our efforts from fighting an outward enemy to doing battle with our own paranoia. Our true war is our struggle against the antagonistic mind. Our true enemy is our propensity to make enemies. The highest form of moral courage requires us to look at ourselves from another perspective, to repent, and to reown our own shadows. True self-knowledge introduces self-doubt into our minds. And self-doubt is a healthy counterbalance to the dogmatic, self-righteous certainty that governs political rhetoric and behavior; it is, therefore, the beginning of compassion.

Thought

1. Paraphrase Keen's thesis. Do you agree with his thesis?
2. Compare Keen's definition of the enemy with your own.
3. According to Keen, why and how are enemies created? Do you agree?
4. "War is an irrational ritual." To what extent is this statement true?
5. "Our natural empathy, our instinct for compassion, is strong." Assess the validity of this statement.

Style and Structure

6. How does Keen circumvent obvious objections to his thesis in the first four paragraphs of the essay?
7. How do the headings serve the purposes of Keen's definition?
8. How has Keen used repetition to strengthen his conclusion?

Response and Extension

9. Find and examine a "face of the enemy" in a recent periodical. Present your findings to the class in an informal speech.
10. Analyze the image of the enemy portrayed in a contemporary film or television series, using the categories that Keen suggests.

The Pleasures of Love

Robertson Davies

- Why do people marry?
- Discuss the qualities of a good marriage.

Let us understand one another at once: I have been asked to discuss the pleasures of love, not its epiphanies, its ecstasies, its disillusionments, its duties, its burdens or its martyrdom—and therefore the sexual aspect of it will get scant attention here. So if you have begun this piece in hope of fanning the flames of your lubricity, be warned in time.

Nor is it my intention to be psychological. I am heartily sick of most of the psychologizing about love that has been going on for the past six hundred years. Everybody wants to say something clever, or profound, about it, and almost everybody has done so. Only look under "Love" in any book of quotations to see how various the opinions are.

Alas, most of this comment is wide of the mark; love, like music and painting, resists analysis in words. It may be described, and some poets and novelists have described it movingly and well; but it does not yield to the theorist. Love is the personal experience of lovers. It must be felt directly.

My own opinion is that it is felt most completely in marriage, or some comparable attachment of long duration. Love takes time. What are called "love affairs" may afford a wide, and in retrospect, illuminating variety of emotions; not only fierce satisfactions and swooning delights, but the horrors of jealousy and the desperation of parting attend them; the hangover from one of these emotional toots may be long and dreadful.

But rarely have the pleasures of love an opportunity to manifest themselves in such riots of passion. Love affairs are for emotional sprinters; the pleasures of love are for the emotional marathoners.

Clearly, then, the pleasures of love are not for the very young. Romeo and Juliet are the accepted pattern of youthful passion. Our hearts go out to their furious abandonment; we are moved to pity by their early death. We do not, unless we are of a saturnine disposition, give a thought to what might have happened if they had been spared for fifty or sixty years together.

Would Juliet have become a worldly nonentity, like her mother? Or would she, egged on by that intolerable old bawd, her nurse, have planted a thicket of horns on the brow of her Romeo?

And he—well, so much would have depended on whether Mercutio had lived; quarrelsome, dashing and detrimental, Mercutio was a man destined to outlive his wit and spend his old age as the Club Bore. No, no; all that Verona crowd were much better off to die young and beautiful.

Passion, so splendid in the young, wants watching as the years wear on. Othello had it, and in middle life he married a young and beautiful girl. What happened? He believed the first scoundrel who hinted that she was unfaithful, and never once took the elementary step of asking her a direct question about the matter.

Passion is a noble thing; I have no use for a man or woman who lacks it; but if we seek the pleasures of love, passion should be occasional, and common sense continual.

Let us get away from Shakespeare. He is the wrong guide in the exploration we have begun. If we talk of the pleasures of love, the best marriage he affords is that of Macbeth and his Lady. Theirs is not the prettiest, nor the highest-hearted, nor the wittiest match in Shakespeare, but unquestionably they knew the pleasures of love.

"My dearest partner of greatness," writes the Thane of Cawdor to his spouse. That is the clue to their relationship. That explains why Macbeth's noblest and most desolate speech follows the news that his Queen is dead.

But who wants to live a modern equivalent of the life of the Macbeths—continuous scheming to reach the Executive Suite enlivened, one presumes, by an occasional Burns Nicht dinner-party, with the ghosts of discredited vice-presidents as uninvited guests.

The pleasures of love are certainly not for the very young, who find a bittersweet pleasure in trying to reconcile two flowering egotisms, nor yet for those who find satisfaction in "affairs." Not that I say a word against young love, or the questings of uncommitted middle-age; but these notions of love correspond to brandy, and we are concerned with something much more like wine.

The pleasures of love are for those who are hopelessly addicted to another living creature. The reasons for such addiction are so many I suspect they are never the same in any two cases.

It includes passion but does not survive by passion; it has its whiffs of the agreeable vertigo of young love, but it is stable more often than dizzy; it is a growing, changing thing, and it is tactful enough to give the addicted parties occasional rests from strong and exhausting feeling of any kind.

"Perfect love sometimes does not come until the first grandchild," says a Welsh proverb. Better far if perfect love does not come at all, but hovers just out of reach. Happy are those who never experience the all-dressed-up-and-no-place-to-go sensation of perfection in love.

What do we seek in love? From my own observation among a group of friends and acquaintances that includes a high proportion of happy marriages, most people are seeking a completion of themselves. Each party to the match has several qualities the other cherishes; the marriage as a whole is decidedly more than the sum of its parts.

Nor are these cherished qualities simply the obvious ones; the reclusive man who marries the gregarious woman, the timid woman who marries the courageous man, the idealist who marries the realist—we can all see these unions: the marriages in which tenderness meets loyalty, where generosity sweetens moroseness, where a sense of beauty eases some aridity of the spirit, are not so easy for outsiders to recognize; the parties themselves may not be fully aware of such elements in a good match.

Often, in choosing a mate, people are unconsciously wise and apprehend what they need to make them greater than they are.

Of course the original disposition of the partners to the marriage points the direction it will take. When Robert Browning married Elizabeth Barrett, the odds were strongly on the side of optimism, in spite of superficial difficulties; when Macbeth and his Lady stepped to the altar, surely some second-sighted Highlander must have shuddered.

If the parties to a marriage have chosen one another unconsciously, knowing only that they will be happier united than apart, they had better set to work as soon as possible to discover why they have married, and to nourish the feeling which has drawn them together.

I am constantly astonished by the people, otherwise intelligent, who think that anything so complex and delicate as a marriage can be left to take care of itself. One sees them fussing about all sorts of lesser concerns, apparently unaware that side by side with them—often in the same bed—a human creature is perishing from lack of affection, of emotional malnutrition.

Such people are living in sin far more truly than the loving, but unwedded, couples whose unions they sometimes scorn. What pleasures are there in these neglected marriages? What pleasure can there be in ramshackle, jerry-built, uncultivated love?

A great part of all the pleasure of love begins, continues and sometimes ends with conversation. A real, enduring love-affair, in marriage and out of it, is an extremely exclusive club of which the entire membership is two co-equal Perpetual Presidents.

In French drama there used to be a character, usually a man, who was the intimate friend of husband and wife, capable of resolving quarrels and keeping the union in repair. I do not believe in such a creature anywhere except behind the footlights. Lovers who need a third party to discuss matters with are in a bad way.

Of course there are marriages that are kept in some sort of rickety shape by a psychiatrist—occasionally by two psychiatrists. But I question if pleasure of the sort I am writing about can exist in such circumstances. The club has become too big.

I do not insist on a union of chatter-boxes, but as you can see I do not believe that still waters run deep; too often I have found that still waters are foul and have mud bottoms. People who love each other should talk to each other; they should confide their real thoughts, their honest emotions, their deepest wishes. How else are they to keep their union in repair?

How else, indeed, are they to discover that they are growing older and enjoying it, which is a very great discovery indeed? How else are they to discover that their union is stronger and richer, not simply because they have shared experience (couples who are professionally at odds, like a Prime Minister and a Leader of the Opposition also share experience, but they are not lovers) but because they are waxing in spirit?

During the last war a cruel epigram was current that Ottawa was full of brilliant men, and the women they had married when they were very young. If the brilliant men had talked more to those women, and the women had replied, the joint impression they made in middle age might not have been so dismal. It is often asserted that sexual compatibility is the foundation of a good marriage, but this pleasure is doomed to wane, whereas a daily affectionate awareness, and a ready tongue last as long as life itself.

It always surprises me, when Prayer Book revision is discussed, that something is not put into the marriage service along these lines—"for the mutual society, help, comfort and unrestricted conversation that one ought to have of the other, both in prosperity and adversity."

Am I then advocating marriages founded on talk? I can hear the puritans, who mistrust conversation as they mistrust all subtle pleasures, tutting their disapproving tuts.

Do I assert that the pleasures of love are no more than the pleasures of conversation? Not at all: I am saying that where the talk is good and copious, love is less likely to wither, or to get out of repair, or to be outgrown, than among the uncommunicative.

For, after all, even lovers live alone much more than we are ready to admit. To keep in constant, sensitive rapport with those we love most, we must open our hearts and our minds. Do this, and the rarest, most delicate pleasures of love will reveal themselves.

Finally, it promotes longevity. Nobody quits a club where the conversation is fascinating, revealing, amusing, various and unexpected until the last possible minute. Love may be snubbed to death: talked to death, never!

Thought

1. Paraphrase and evaluate Davies' definition of love.
2. What does Davies exclude from the pleasures of love? Do you agree with his exclusions? Explain.
3. Examine Davies' reasons why some people are "hopelessly addicted to another living creature."
4. How does Davies justify the central importance of conversation in a loving relationship?

Style and Structure

5. How does Davies engage the reader in his first three paragraphs?
6. Explain Davies' use of metaphor in the fourth and fifth paragraphs.
7. By selecting at least three words or phrases from the essay, characterize the tone of Davies' discussion of *Romeo and Juliet.*
8. Select and discuss several examples of Davies' use of formal and informal diction. What general statement can you make about his vocabulary?

Response and Extension

9. Using the argument that Davies presents, write a letter counselling an imaginary couple who are contemplating divorce.
10. Write an editorial giving your definition of marriage or a "comparable attachment of long duration."

Marriage Is Belonging

Katherine Anne Porter

• What advice would you give a friend who is about to marry?

Having never written a word about marriage, so far as I remember, and being now at the point where I have learned better than to have any theories about it, if I ever had; and believing as I do that most of the stuff written and talked about it is more or less nonsense; and having little hope that I shall add luster to the topic, it is only logical and natural that I should venture to write a few words on the subject.

My theme is marriage as the art of belonging—which should not be confused with possessing—all too often the art, or perhaps only the strategy, and a risky one, of surrendering gracefully with an air of pure disinterestedness as much of your living self as you can spare without incurring total extinction; in return for which you will, at least in theory, receive a more than compensatory share of another life, the life in fact presumably dearest to you, equally whittled down in your favor to the barest margin of survival.

This arrangement with variations to suit the circumstances is of course the basis of many contracts besides that of marriage; but nowhere more than in marriage does the real good of the relationship depend on intangibles not named in the bond.

The trouble with me is—always was—that if you say "marriage" to me, instantly the word translates itself into "love," for only in such terms can I grasp the idea at all, or make any sense of it. The two are hopelessly associated, or rather identified, in my mind; that is to say, love is the only excuse for marriage, if any excuse is necessary. I often feel one should be offered. Love without marriage can sometimes be very awkward for all concerned; but marriage without love simply removes that institution from the territory of the humanly admissible, to my mind. Love is a state in which one lives who loves, and whoever loves has given himself away; love then, and not marriage, is belonging. Marriage is the public declaration of a man and a woman that they have formed a secret alliance, with the intention to belong to, and share with each other, a mystical estate; mystical exactly in the sense that the real experience cannot be communicated to others, nor explained even to oneself on rational grounds.

By love let me make it clear, I do not refer only to that ecstatic reciprocal cannibalism which goes popularly under the name, and which is indeed commonly one of the earliest biological symptoms (Boy Eats Girl and vice versa), for, like all truly mystical things, love is rooted deeply and rightly in this world and this flesh. This phase is natural, dangerous but not necessarily fatal; so remarkably educational it would be a great pity to miss it; further, of great importance, for the flesh in real love is one of the many bridges to the spirit; still, a phase only, which being passed is too often mistaken for the whole thing, and the end of it. This is an error based on lack of imagination, or the simple incapacity for further and deeper exploration of life, there being always on hand great numbers of people who are unwilling or unable to grow up, no matter what happens to them. It leads to early divorce, or worse. Like that young man whose downward career began with mere murder, this error can lead to infidelity, lying, eavesdropping, gambling, drinking, and finally to procrastination and incivility. These two last can easily have destroyed more marriages than any amount of murder, or even lying.

Let us recall a few generalities about marriage in its practical aspects which are common knowledge, such as: it is one of the most prevalent conditions of the human adult, heading the list of vital statistics, I believe. It has been made very easy to assume, and fairly easy in the legal sense, at least, to abandon; and it is famous for its random assortment of surprises of every kind—leaf-covered booby traps, spiders lurking in cups, pots of gold under rainbows, triplets, poltergeists in the stair closet, and flights of cupids lolling on the breakfast table—anything can happen. Every young married pair believes their marriage is going to be quite different from the others, and they are right—it always is. The task of regulating its unruly impulses is a thorn in the souls of theologians, its social needs and uses the insoluble riddle of law-makers. Through all ages known to man almost everybody, even those who wouldn't be seen dead wearing a wedding ring, having agreed that somehow, in some way, at some time or another, marriage has simply got to be made to work better than it does, or ever has, for that matter. Yet on the whole, my guess is that it works about as well as any other human institution, and rather better than a great many. The drawback is, it is the merciless revealer, the great white searchlight turned on the darkest places of human nature; it demands of all who enter it the two most difficult achievements possible: that each must be honest with himself, and faithful to another. I am speaking here only of the internal reality of marriage, not its legal or even its social aspects.

In its present form it is comparatively modern. As an idea, it must have begun fairly soon after the human male discovered his highly important role in the bringing forth of young. For countless aeons, we are told by those who pretend to know, it was believed that the powers of generation were vested in women alone, people having never been very bright about sex, right from the start. When men at last discovered, who knows how? that they were fathers, their pride in their discovery must have been equaled only by their indignation at having worshiped women as vessels of the Great Mystery when all along they should have been worshiping themselves. Pride and wrath and no doubt the awful new problem of what to do with the children, which had never bothered them before, drove them on to an infinite number of complicated and contradictory steps toward getting human affairs on a sounder basis. And, after all this time (skipping lightly over the first few hundred thousand years of total confusion), in our fine big new busy Western world, we have succeeded in establishing not only as the ideal, but in religious and legal fact (if not altogether in practice), as the very crown and glory of human ties, a one-man-one-woman-until-death sort of marriage, rivaling the swans for purity, with a ritual oath exchanged not only to stick to each other through thick and thin, to practice perfect fidelity, flawless forbearance, a modified bodily servitude, but to love each other dearly and kindly to the end.

All this is to be accomplished in a physical situation of the direst intimacy, in which all claims to the most ordinary privacy may be disregarded by either, or both. I shall not attempt to catalogue the daily accounting for acts, words, states of feeling and even thoughts, the perpetual balance and check between individual wills and points of view, the unbelievable amount of tact, intelligence, flexibility, generosity, and God knows what, it requires for two people to go on growing together and in the same directions instead of cracking up and falling apart.

Take the single point of fidelity: It is very hard to be entirely faithful, even to things, ideas, above all, persons one loves. There is no such thing as perfect faithfulness any more than there is perfect love or perfect beauty. But it is fun trying. And if I say faithfulness consists of a great many things beside the physical, never let it be dreamed that I hold with the shabby nonsense that physical infidelity is a mere peccadillo beneath the notice of enlightened minds. Physical infidelity is the signal, the notice given, that all the fidelities are undermined. It is complete betrayal of the very principle on which love and marriage are based, and besides, a vulgar handing over of one's partner to public shame. It is exactly as stupid as that, to say nothing more.

Yet every day quite by the thousands delightfully honest young couples, promising, capable, sometimes gifted, but in no way superhuman, leap gaily into marriage—a condition which, for even reasonable success and happiness (both words seem rather trivial in this connection), would tax the virtues and resources and staying powers of a regiment of angels. But what else would you suggest that they do?

Then there come the children. Gladly, willingly (if you do not think so, I refer you to the birth records of this country for the past ten years. There haven't been so many young wives having so many babies so fast for at least four generations!) these pairs proceed to populate their houses, or flats—often very small flats, and mother with a job she means to keep, too—with perfect strangers, often hostile, whose habits even to the most adoring gaze are often messy and unattractive. They lie flat on their noses at first in what appears to be a drunken slumber, then flat on their backs kicking and screaming, demanding impossibilities in a foreign language. They are human nature in essence, without conscience, without pity, without love, without a trace of consideration for others, just one seething cauldron of primitive appetites and needs; and what do they really need? We are back where we started. They need love, first; without it everything worth saving is lost or damaged in them; and they have to be taught love, pity, conscience, courage—everything. And what becomes of them? If they are lucky, among all the million possibilities of their fates, along with the innumerable employments, careers, talents, ways of life, they will learn the nature of love, and they will marry and have children.

If this all sounds a little monotonous, and gregarious, well, sometimes it is, and most people like that sort of thing. They always have. It is hardly possible to exaggerate the need of a human being, not a madman, or a saint, or a beast, or a self-alienated genius who is all of these in one, and therefore the scapegoat for all the rest, to live at peace—and by peace I mean in reconciliation, not easy contentment—with another human being, and with that one in a group or society where he feels he belongs. The best, the very best, of all these relationships is that one in marriage between a man and a woman who are good lovers, good friends, and good parents; who belong to each other, and to their children, and whose children belong to them: that is the meaning of the blood tie that binds them, and may bind them sometimes to the bone. Children cut their teeth on their parents and their parents cut their wisdom teeth on each other: that is what they are there for. It is never really dull, and can sometimes be very memorably exciting for everybody. In any case, the blood-bond, however painful, is the condition of human life in this world, the absolute point of all departure and return. The ancient biological laws are still in force, the difference being merely in the way human beings regard them, and though I am not one to say all change is progress, in this one thing, a kind of freedom and ease of mind between men and women in marriage—or at least the possibility of it, change has been all for the better. At least they are able now to fight out their differences on something nearer equal terms.

We have the bad habit, some of us, of looking back to a time—almost any time will do—when society was stable and orderly, family ties stronger and deeper, love more lasting and faithful, and so on. Let me be your Cassandra prophesying after the fact, and a long study of the documents in the case: it was never true, that is, no truer than it is now. Above all, it was not true of domestic life in the nineteenth century. Then, as now, it was just as good in individual instances as the married pairs involved were able to make it, privately, between themselves. The less attention they paid to what they were expected to think and feel about marriage, and the more attention to each other as loved and loving, the better they did, for themselves and for everybody. The laws of public decorum were easy to observe, for they had another and better understanding. The Victorian marriage feather bed was in fact set upon the shaky foundation of the wavering human heart, the inconsistent human mind, and was the roiling hotbed of every dislocation and disorder not only in marriage but all society, which we of the past two generations have lived through. Yet in love—this is what I have been talking about all the time—a certain number of well-endowed spirits, and there are surprisingly quite a lot of them in every generation, have always been able to take their world in stride, to live and die together, and to keep all their strange marriage vows not because they spoke them, but because like centuries of lovers before them, they were prepared to live them in the first place.

Example: A certain woman was apparently a prisoner for life in several ways: already thirty-five or -six years old, supposed to be an incurable invalid, whose father had forbidden any of his children to marry; and above all, a poet at a time when literary women were regarded as monsters, almost. Yet she was able to write, in the first flush of a bride's joy: "He preferred...of free and deliberate choice, to be allowed to sit only an hour a day by my side, to the fulfillment of the brightest dream which should exclude me in any possible world."

This could be illusion, but the proof of reality came fifteen years later. Just after her death her husband wrote to a friend: "Then came what my heart will keep till I see her again and longer—the most perfect expression of her love to me within my whole knowledge of her. Always smilingly, and happily, and with a face like a girl's; and in a few minutes she died in my arms, her head on my cheek."

If you exclaim that this is not fair, for, after all, these two were, of course, the Robert Brownings, I can only reply that it is because I sincerely believe they were not so very special that I cite them. Don't be thrown off by that lyrical nineteenth-century speech, nor their fearless confidence not only in their own feelings, but the sympathy of their friends; it is the kind of love that makes real marriage, and there is more of it in the world than you might think, though the ways of expressing it follow the fashions of the times; and we certainly do not find much trace of it in our contemporary literature. It is *very* old-style, and it was, long before the Brownings. It is new, too, it is the very newest thing, every day renewed in an endless series of those fortunate people who may not have one point in common with the Brownings except that they know, or are capable of learning, the nature of love, and of living by it.

Thought

1. Distinguish between "belonging" and "possessing" as Porter defines them.

2. Paraphrase Porter's statement: "the flesh in real love is one of the many bridges to the spirit; still, a phase only, which being passed is too often mistaken for the whole thing, and the end of it." Do you agree or disagree with Porter? Explain.

3. According to Porter, what is the drawback of marriage? Do you agree with her? Explain.

4. Summarize and assess Porter's thoughts on intimacy and faithfulness.

Style and Structure

5. Select two short passages and analyze Porter's sentence structure. Comment upon the appropriateness of her sentence structure in defining her subject.

6. Quote several sentences or phrases which illustrate Porter's wit. Why are they good examples?

7. What is the relationship between the concluding four paragraphs and the rest of the essay?

Response and Extension

8. Write an essay using as your thesis the idea contained in the following sentence: "In any case, the blood-bond, however painful, is the condition of human life in this world, the absolute point of all departure and return."

9. Interview a person who was raised in a culture in which marriages are "arranged." Present a report defining that culture's practice of arranging marriages.

Unit Synthesis

1. Using Keen's definitions of the enemy, analyze the enmity between the protagonist and antagonists in a novel such as *The Wars* by Timothy Findley; *A Separate Peace* by John Knowles; *Lord of The Flies* by William Golding; *A Farewell To Arms* by Ernest Hemingway.

2. Applying what you have learned in Keen's essay, examine Shakespeare's "propaganda techniques" in plays such as *Richard The Third, Hamlet, King Lear, Romeo and Juliet.*

3. Compare and contrast the essays by Porter and Davies included in this chapter in terms of thought and style.

4. With references to the definitions suggested by Davies and Porter, analyze the ways in which marriage is portrayed in a popular television series.

WRITING TO EXPLAIN

Explanations state relationships among individuals, ideas and events.

Judy Syfers explains herself in terms of her relationships with others. "I belong to that classification of people known as wives. I am A Wife. And, not altogether incidentally, I am a mother."

Judy Stoffman dismisses the commonplace comparison of the human body to a machine. "The belief that the body is a machine whose parts wear out is erroneous," she writes, "for the machine does not have the body's capacity for self-repair."

John David Sinclair's essay, "The Hardware of The Brain," deals with the much-debated relationship which exists between two quite dissimilar systems, the organic and the inorganic. He concludes his explanation with the view that "useful developments are more likely to come from the interactions and cooperation between these two essentially complementary systems."

In "The Winter of Man," Loren Eiseley explains the fear that underlies the relationship between human beings and nature. "We fear the awesome powers we have lifted out of nature and cannot return to her."

Peter Sypnowich explains some of the relationships which exist between language and nationality: "That Canadian English is a poor vehicle for nationalism is evident in the paucity of purely Canadian words." Further, he explains that "written language has always been and always will be a representation of speech. If you don't say it, you can't write it." He concludes, "If we are going to write the language of the future, we will close our ears to the scratching of quill pens and the cries of the pedants. We will listen to our own voices."

An explanatory essay ultimately does more than provide information about a relationship. It invites inferences. It informs judgement.

Why I Want a Wife

Judy Syfers

- Research the etymology of the words "husband," "wife," "lord," "lady."
- What do the original meanings of these words reveal about the historical relationships between men and women?

I belong to that classification of people known as wives. I am A Wife. And, not altogether incidentally, I am a mother.

Not too long ago a male friend of mine appeared on the scene fresh from a recent divorce. He had one child, who is, of course, with his ex-wife. He is looking for another wife. As I thought about him while I was ironing one evening, it suddenly occurred to me that I, too, would like to have a wife. Why do I want a wife?

I would like to go back to school so that I can become economically independent, support myself, and, if need be, support those dependent upon me. I want a wife who will work and send me to school. And while I am going to school I want a wife to take care of my children. I want a wife to keep track of the children's doctor and dentist appointments. And to keep track of mine, too. I want a wife to make sure my children eat properly and are kept clean. I want a wife who will wash the children's clothes and keep them mended. I want a wife who is a good nurturant attendant to my children, who arranges for their schooling, makes sure that they have an adequate social life with their peers, takes them to the park, the zoo, etc. I want a wife who takes care of the children when they are sick, a wife who arranges to be around when the children need special care, because, of course, I cannot miss classes at school. My wife must arrange to lose time at work and not lose the job. It may mean a small cut in my wife's income from time to time, but I guess I can tolerate that. Needless to say, my wife will arrange and pay for the care of the children while my wife is working.

I want a wife who will take care of *my* physical needs. I want a wife who will keep my house clean. A wife who will pick up after my children, a wife who will pick up after me. I want a wife who will keep my clothes clean, ironed, mended, replaced when need be, and who will see to it that my personal things are kept in their proper place so that I can find what I need the minute I need it. I want a wife who cooks the meals, a wife who is a *good* cook. I want a wife who will plan the menus, do the necessary grocery shopping, prepare the meals, serve them pleasantly, and then do the cleaning up while I do my studying. I want a wife who will care for me when I am sick and sympathize with my pain and loss of time from school. I want a wife to go along when our family takes a vacation so that someone can continue to care for me and my children when I need a rest and change of scene.

I want a wife who will not bother me with rambling complaints about a wife's duties. But I want a wife who will listen to me when I feel the need to explain a rather difficult point I have come across in my course of studies. And I want a wife who will type my papers for me when I have written them.

I want a wife who will take care of the details of my social life. When my wife and I are invited out by my friends, I want a wife who will take care of the babysitting arrangements. When I meet people at school that I like and want to entertain, I want a wife who will have the house clean, will prepare a special meal, serve it to me and my friends, and not interrupt when I talk about things that interest me and my friends. I want a wife who will have arranged that the children are fed and ready for bed before my guests arrive so that the children do not bother us. I want a wife who takes care of the needs of my guests so that they feel comfortable, who makes sure that they have an ashtray, that they are passed the hors d'oeuvres, that they are offered a second helping of the food, that their wine glasses are replenished when necessary, that their coffee is served to them as they like it. And I want a wife who knows that sometimes I need a night out by myself.

I want a wife who is sensitive to my sexual needs, a wife who makes love passionately and eagerly when I feel like it, a wife who makes sure that I am satisfied. And, of course, I want a wife who will not demand sexual attention when I am not in the mood for it. I want a wife who assumes the complete responsibility for birth control, because I do not want more children. I want a wife who will remain sexually faithful to me so that I do not have to clutter up my intellectual life with jealousies. And I want a wife who understands that *my* sexual needs may entail more than strict adherence to monogamy. I must, after all, be able to relate to people as fully as possible.

If, by chance, I find another person more suitable as a wife than the wife I already have, I want the liberty to replace my present wife with another one. Naturally, I will expect a fresh, new life; my wife will take the children and be solely responsible for them so that I am left free.

When I am through with school and have a job, I want my wife to quit working and remain at home so that my wife can more fully and completely take care of a wife's duties.

My God, who *wouldn't* want a wife?

Thought

1. Prove that Syfers' use of the word "wife" is entirely consistent with its original meaning.
2. To what extent do you think this essay presents an accurate assessment of the relationship between married men and women?

Style and Structure

3. Judge the effectiveness of the first two paragraphs in establishing the essay as an explanation.
4. Characterize the persona Syfers adopts in the body of the essay.
5. Who is the intended audience and how does the author expect that audience to respond?
6. How does the author convey her anger without alienating her audience?
7. What effects does Syfers achieve by her repetition of "I want a wife who…"?

Response and Extension

8. Write an essay entitled "Why I Want (Don't Want) a Husband."
9. Write a dialogue that depicts the different attitudes in a family or community toward the relationship between husbands and wives.

The Way of All Flesh

Judy Stoffman

- What is aging?
- At what age is one no longer young? Explain.
- Why do some people fear old age? Explain.

When a man of 25 is told that aging is inexorable, inevitable, universal, he will nod somewhat impatiently at being told something so obvious. In fact, he has little idea of the meaning of the words. It has nothing to do with him. Why should it? He has had no tangible evidence yet that his body, as the poet Rilke said, enfolds old age and death as the fruit enfolds a stone.

The earliest deposits of fat in the aorta, the trunk artery carrying blood away from the heart, occur in the eighth year of life, but who can peer into his own aorta at this first sign of approaching debility? The young man has seen old people but he secretly believes himself to be the exception on whom the curse will never fall. "Never will the skin of my neck hang loose. My grip will never weaken. I will stand tall and walk with long strides as long as I live." The young girl scarcely pays attention to her clothes, she scorns makeup. Her confidence in her body is boundless; smooth skin and a flat stomach will compensate, she knows, for any lapses in fashion or grooming. She stays up all night, as careless of her energy as of her looks, believing both will last forever.

In our early 20s, the lung capacity, the rapidity of motor responses and physical endurance are at their peak. This is the athlete's finest hour. Cindy Nicholas of Toronto was 19 when she first swam the English Channel in both directions. The tennis star Bjorn Borg was 23 when he triumphed this year at Wimbledon for the fourth time.

It is not only *athletic* prowess that is at its height between 20 and 30. James Boswell, writing in his journal in 1763 after he had finally won the favors of the actress Louisa, has left us this happy description of the sexual prowess of a 23-year-old: "I was in full glow of health and my bounding blood beat quick in high alarms. Five times was I fairly lost in supreme rapture. Louisa was madly fond of me; she declared I was a prodigy, and asked me if this was extraordinary in human nature. I said twice as much might be, but this was not, although in my own mind I was somewhat proud of my performance.''

In our early 30s we are dumbfounded to discover the first grey hair at the temples. We pull out the strange filament and look at it closely, trying to grasp its meaning. It means simply that the pigment has disappeared from the hair shaft, never to return. It means also—but this thought we push away—that in 20 years or so we'll relinquish our identity as a blonde or a redhead. By 57, one out of four people is completely grey. Of all the changes wrought by time this is the most harmless, except to our vanity.

In this decade one also begins to notice the loss of upper register hearing, that is, the responsiveness to high frequency tones, but not all the changes are for the worse, not yet. Women don't reach their sexual prime until about 38, because their sexual response is learned rather than innate. The hand grip of both sexes increases in strength until 35, and intellectual powers are never stronger than at that age. There is a sense in the 30s of hitting your stride, of coming into your own. When Sigmund Freud was 38 an older colleague, Josef Breuer, wrote: "Freud's intellect is soaring at its highest. I gaze after him as a hen at a hawk."

Gail Sheehy in her book *Passages* calls the interval between 35 and 45 the Deadline Decade. It is the time we begin to sense danger. The body continually flashes us signals that time is running out. We must perform our quaint deeds, keep our promises, get on with our allotted tasks.

Signal: The woman attempts to become pregnant at 40 and finds she cannot. Though she menstruates each month, menstruation being merely the shedding of the inner lining of the womb, she may not be ovulating regularly.

Signal: Both men and women discover that, although they have not changed their eating habits over the years, they are much heavier than formerly. The man is paunchy around the waist; the woman no longer has those slim thighs and slender arms. A 120-pound woman needs 2,000 calories daily to maintain her weight when she is 25, 1,700 to maintain the same weight at 45, and only 1,500 calories at 65. A 170-pound man needs 3,100 calories daily at 25, 300 fewer a day at 45 and 450 calories fewer still at 65. This decreasing calorie need signals that the body consumes its fuel ever more slowly; the cellular fires are damped and our sense of energy diminishes.

In his mid-40s the man notices he can no longer run up the stairs three at a time. He is more easily winded and his joints are not as flexible as they once were. The strength of his hands has declined somewhat. The man feels humiliated: "I will not let this happen to me. I will turn back the tide and master my body." He starts going to the gym, playing squash, lifting weights. He takes up jogging. Though he may find it neither easy nor pleasant, terror drives him past pain. A regular exercise program can retard some of the symptoms of aging by improving the circulation and increasing the lung capacity, thereby raising our stamina and energy level, but no amount of exercise will make a 48-year-old 26 again. Take John Keeley of Mystic, Connecticut. In 1957, when he was 26, he won the Boston marathon with a time of 2:20. This year he is fit and 48 and says he is as fiercely competitive as ever, yet it took him almost 30 minutes longer to run the same marathon.

In the middle of the fourth decade, the man whose eyesight has always been good will pick up a book and notice that he is holding it farther from his face than usual. The condition is presbyopia, a loss of the flexibility of the lens which makes adjustment from distant to near vision increasingly difficult. It's harder now to zoom in for a closeup. It also takes longer for the eyes to recover from glare; between 16 and 90, recovery time from exposure to glare is doubled every 13 years.

In our 50s, we notice that food is less and less tasty; our taste buds are starting to lose their acuity. The aged Queen Victoria was wont to complain that strawberries were not as sweet as when she was a girl.

Little is known about the causes of aging. We do not know if we are born with a biochemical messenger programed to keep the cells and tissues alive, a messenger that eventually gets lost, or if there is a 'death hormone,' absent from birth but later secreted by the thymus or by the mysterious pineal gland, or if, perhaps, aging results from a fatal flaw in the body's immunity system. The belief that the body is a machine whose parts wear out is erroneous, for the machine does not have the body's capacity for self-repair.

"A man is as old as his arteries," observed Sir William Osler. From the 50s on, there's a progressive hardening and narrowing of the arteries due to the gradual lifelong accumulation of calcium and fats along the arterial walls. Arteriosclerosis eventually affects the majority of the population in the affluent countries of the West. Lucky the man or woman who, through a combination of good genes and good nutrition, can escape it, for it is the most evil change of all. As the flow of blood carrying oxygen and nutrients to the muscles, the brain, the kidneys and other organs diminishes, these organs begin to starve. Although all aging organs lose weight, there is less shrinkage of organs such as the liver and kidneys, the cells of which regenerate, than there is shrinkage of the brain and the muscles, the cells of which, once lost, are lost forever.

For the woman it is now an ordeal to be asked her age. There is a fine tracery of lines around her eyes, a furrow in her brow even when she smiles. The bloom is off her cheeks. Around the age of 50 she will buy her last box of sanitary pads. The body's production of estrogen and progesterone which govern menstruation (and also help to protect her from heart attack and the effects of stress) will have ceased almost completely. She may suffer palpitations, suddenly break into a sweat; her moods may shift abruptly. She looks in the mirror and asks, "Am I still a woman?" Eventually she becomes reconciled to her new self and even acknowledges its advantages: no more fears about pregnancy. "In any case," she laughs, "I still have not bad legs."

The man, too, will undergo a change. One night in his early 50s he has some trouble achieving a complete erection, and his powers of recovery are not what they once were. Whereas at 20 he was ready to make love again less than half an hour after doing so, it may now take two hours or more; he was not previously aware that his level of testosterone, the male hormone, has been gradually declining since the age of 20. He may develop headaches, be unable to sleep, become anxious about his performance, anticipate failure and so bring on what is called secondary impotence—impotence of psychological rather than physical origin. According to Masters and Johnson, 25 percent of all men are impotent by 65 and 50 percent by 75, yet this cannot be called an inevitable feature of aging. A loving, undemanding partner and a sense of confidence can do wonders. "The susceptibility of the human male to the power of suggestion with regard to his sexual prowess," observe Masters and Johnson, "is almost unbelievable."

After the menopause, the woman ages more rapidly. Her bones start to lose calcium, becoming brittle and porous. The walls of the vagina become thinner and drier; sexual intercourse now may be painful unless her partner is slow and gentle. The sweat glands begin to atrophy and the sebaceous glands that lubricate the skin decline; the complexion becomes thinner and drier and wrinkles appear around the mouth. The skin, which in youth varies from about one-fiftieth of an inch on the eyelids to about a third of an inch on the palms and the soles of the feet, loses 50 percent of its thickness between the ages of 20 and 80. The woman no longer buys sleeveless dresses and avoids shorts. The girl who once disdained cosmetics is now a woman whose dressing table is covered with lotions, night creams and makeup.

Perhaps no one has written about the sensation of nearing 60 with more brutal honesty than the French novelist Simone de Beauvoir: "While I was able to look at my face without displeasure, I gave it no thought. I loathe my appearance now: the eyebrows slipping down toward the eyes, the bags underneath, the excessive fullness of the cheeks and the air of sadness around the mouth that wrinkles always bring. . . . Death is no longer a brutal event in the far distance; it haunts my sleep.''

In his early 60s the man's calves are shrunken, his muscles stringy looking. The legs of the woman, too, are no longer shapely. Both start to lose their sense of smell and both lose most of the hair in the pubic area and the underarms. Hair, however, may make its appearance in new places, such as the woman's chin. Liver spots appear on the hands, the arms, the face; they are made of coagulated melanin, the coloring matter of the skin. The acid secretions of the stomach decrease, making digestion slow and more difficult.

Halfway through the 60s comes compulsory retirement for most men and working women, forcing upon the superannuated worker the realization that society now views him as useless and unproductive. The man who formerly gave orders to a staff of 20 now finds himself underfoot as his wife attempts to clean the house or get the shopping done. The woman fares a little better since there is a continuity in her pattern of performing a myriad of essential household tasks. Now they must both set new goals or see themselves wither mentally. The unsinkable American journalist I.F. Stone, when he retired in 1971 from editing *I.F. Stone's Weekly*, began to teach himself Greek and is now reading Plato in the original. When Somerset Maugham read that the Roman senator Cato the Elder learned Greek when he was 80, he remarked: ''Old age is ready to undertake tasks that youth shirked because they would take too long.''

However active we are, the fact of old age can no longer be evaded from about 65 onward. Not everyone is as strong minded about this as de Beauvoir. When she made public in her memoirs her horror at her own deterioration, her readers were scandalized. She received hundreds of letters telling her that there is no such thing as old age, that some are just younger than others. Repeatedly she heard the hollow reassurance, ''You're as young as you feel.'' But she considers this a lie. Our subjective reality, our inner sense of self, is not the only reality. There is also an objective reality, how we are seen by society. We receive our revelation of old age from others. The woman whose figure is still trim may sense that a man is following her in the street; drawing abreast, the man catches sight of her face—and hurries on. The man of 68 may be told by a younger woman to whom he is attracted: ''You remind me of my father.''

Madame de Sévigné, the 17th-century French writer, struggled to rid herself of the illusion of perpetual youth. At 63 she wrote: ''I have been dragged to this inevitable point where old age must be undergone: I see it there before me; I have reached it; and I should at least like so to arrange matters that I do not move on, that I do not travel further along this path of the infirmities, pains, losses of memory and the disfigurement. But I hear a voice saying: 'You must go along, whatever you may say; or indeed if you will not then you must die, which is an extremity from which nature recoils.'"

Now the man and the woman have their 70th birthday party. It is a sad affair because so many of their friends are missing, felled by strokes, heart attacks or cancers. Now the hands of the clock begin to race. The skeleton continues to degenerate from loss of calcium. The spine becomes compressed and there is a slight stoop nothing can prevent. Inches are lost from one's height. The joints may become thickened and creaking; in the morning the woman can't seem to get moving until she's had a hot bath. She has osteoarthritis. This, like the other age-related diseases, arteriosclerosis and diabetes, can and should be treated but it can never be cured. The nails, particularly the toenails, become thick and lifeless because the circulation in the lower limbs is now poor. The man has difficulty learning new things because of the progressive loss of neurons from the brain. The woman goes to the store and forgets what she has come to buy. The two old people are often constipated because the involuntary muscles are weaker now. To make it worse, their children are always saying, "Sit down, rest, take it easy." Their digestive tract would be toned up if they went for a long walk or even a swim, although they feel a little foolish in bathing suits.

In his late 70s, the man develops glaucoma, pressure in the eyeball caused by the failure of the aqueous humour to drain away; this can now be treated with a steroid related to cortisone. The lenses in the eyes of the woman may thicken and become fibrous, blurring her vision. She has cataracts, but artificial lenses can now be implanted using cryosurgery. There is no reason to lose one's sight just as there's no reason to lose one's teeth; regular, lifelong dental care can prevent tooth loss. What can't be prevented is the yellowing of teeth, brought about by the shrinking of the living chamber within the tooth which supplies the outer enamel with moisture.

Between 75 and 85 the body loses most of its subcutaneous fat. On her 80th birthday the woman's granddaughter embraces her and marvels: "How thin and frail and shrunken she is! Could this narrow, bony chest be the same warm, firm bosom to which she clasped me as a child?" Her children urge her to eat but she has no enjoyment of food now. Her mouth secretes little saliva, so she has difficulty tasting and swallowing. The loss of fat and shrinking muscles in the 80s diminish the body's capacity for homeostasis, that is, righting any physiological imbalance. The old man, if he is cold, can barely shiver (shivering serves to restore body heat). If he lives long enough, the man will have an enlarged prostate which causes the urinary stream to slow to a trickle. The man and the woman probably both wear hearing aids now; without a hearing aid, they hear vowels clearly but not consonants; if someone says "fat," they think they've heard the word "that."

At 80, the speed of nerve impulses is 10 percent less than it was at 25, the kidney filtration rate is down by 30 percent, the pumping efficiency of the heart is only 60 percent of what it was, and the maximum breathing capacity, 40 percent.

The old couple is fortunate in still being able to express physically the love they've built up over a lifetime. The old man may be capable of an erection once or twice a week (Charlie Chaplin fathered the last of his many children when he was 81), but he rarely has the urge to climax. When he does, he sometimes has the sensation of seepage rather than a triumphant explosion. Old people who say they are relieved that they are now free of the torments of sexual desire are usually the ones who found sex a troublesome function all their lives; those who found joy and renewal in the act will cling to their libido. Many older writers and artists have expressed the conviction that continued sexuality is linked to continued creativity: "There was a time when I was cruelly tormented, indeed obsessed by desire," wrote the novelist André Gide at the age of 73, "and I prayed, 'Oh let the moment come when my subjugated flesh will allow me to give myself entirely to . . .' But to what? To art? To pure thought? To God? How ignorant I was! How mad! It was the same as believing that the flame would burn brighter in a lamp with no oil left. Even today it is my carnal self that feeds the flame, and now I pray that I may retain carnal desire until I die."

Aging, says an American gerontologist, "is not a simple slope which everyone slides down at the same speed; it is a flight of irregular stairs down which some journey more quickly than others." Now we arrive at the bottom of the stairs. The old man and the old woman whose progress we have been tracing will die either of a cancer (usually of the lungs, bowel or intestines) or of a stroke, a heart attack or in consequence of a fall. The man slips in the bathroom and breaks his thigh bone. But worse than the fracture is the enforced bed rest in the hospital which will probably bring on bed sores, infections, further weakening of the muscles and finally, what Osler called "an old man's best friend": pneumonia. At 25 we have so much vitality that if a little is sapped by illness, there is still plenty left over. At 85 a little is all we have.

And then the light goes out.

The sheet is pulled over the face.

In the last book of Marcel Proust's remarkable work *Remembrance of Things Past*, the narrator, returning after a long absence from Paris, attends a party of his friends throughout which he has the impression of being at a masked ball: "I did not understand why I could not immediately recognize the master of the house, and the guests, who seemed to have made themselves up, in a way that completely changed their appearance. The Prince had rigged himself up with a white beard and what looked like leaden soles which made his feet drag heavily. A name was mentioned to me and I was dumbfounded at the thought that it applied to the blonde waltzing girl I had once known and to the stout, white haired lady now walking just in front of me. We did not see our own appearance, but each like a facing mirror, saw the other's." The narrator is overcome by a simple but powerful truth: the old are not a different species. "It is out of young men who last long enough," wrote Proust, "that life makes its old men."

The wrinkled old man who lies with the sheet over his face was once the young man who vowed, "My grip will never weaken. I will walk with long strides and stand tall as long as I live." The young man who believed himself to be the exception.

Thought

1. List three statements from the essay which disturb you. Explain why they disturb you.

2. Paraphrase those statements which express a positive attitude toward aging.

3. What aspects of human aging are not addressed in this essay? Suggest reasons for these omissions.

Style and Structure

4. What is the organizing principle of this essay? How does this organizing principle serve the author's purpose?

5. Why has the author used so many quotations? What do these quotations have in common?

Response and Extension

6. "Old age is ready to undertake tasks that youth shirked because they would take too long." Write an explanatory essay which clarifies the meaning of this statement.
7. Compose a short editorial which attempts to account for North American society's obsession with youthfulness.
8. Debate the following statement: "We receive our revelation of old age from others."

The Hardware of the Brain

John David Sinclair

- In groups, discuss the ways in which computers directly affect your life.
- Do you think that "artificial intelligence" will surpass human intelligence? Explain.
- Should limitations be imposed on artificial intelligence?

Computer people often are asked whether computers will ever be able to think the way humans do. Their answers are interesting and useful, but I'd like to tackle the question from the point of view of a biologist.

I believe we can get close to an answer by examining how our brains work and how computers work. It turns out that the basic units used for constructing brains and computers behave quite differently. The basic units of a computer are the transistors, which act as switches that can either be closed, in which case electricity flows through them, or open, in which case the signal does not get through. These two states correspond to the 1 and 0 in the binary counting system that computers use.

The basic units in the brain are generally believed to be the synapses, which also act like switches. The circuitry in the brain depends on which of these synaptic switches are open and closed. Change the switches and you change the circuitry; this is turn changes the way the brain functions and thus changes the behavior of the creature possessing the brain. Changing switches is thus generally believed to form the basis for altering the programs in the brain and for storing information, just as it is in the computer.

The first major difference between transistors and synapses is that synapses have more than just the two states—closed and open—used by computers. Synapses can be partly open and partly closed, so that there is only a certain probability that a signal will get through. Therefore, in addition to the states equivalent to 1 and 0 of the binary system, synapses can have intermediate values, such as nine-tenths and two-tenths. These values are usually called the "strength" of the synapses.

Synapses are thus more like loose connections than good switches. Having a brain with about 100 trillion loose connections may be partly responsible for our sometimes fuzzy thinking.

Another difference between transistors and synapses is that the multitude of transistors in the computer are used only for storing information. In the brain, synapses function both as memory storage units and as microprocessors. Each synapse performs two types of processing. In a simple manner, the synapse acts to process the signals by summing signals over time. This means that a relatively weak synapse may not act on a single isolated impulse, but if several impulses arrive in short succession, the synapse will produce an output. Synapses also summate spatially: An input to one synapse may produce no output, but several inputs arriving at about the same time at different synapses on the same neuron yield an output. In addition to summing impulses temporally and spatially, the synapse's other mode of processing is to change its strength as a result of experience. This is the main reason for both the power and the weakness of the brain, relative to computers.

In the computer, the functions of memory and processing are separate. A computer has only one central processing unit which can do only one thing at a time. Information must be queued up in one long string to be processed. The brain, however, with a microprocessor in each synapse, can process a huge number of strings of information at the same time. The brain has to pay for this advantage: It uses all of its units as processors and has none left over for just storing information. Consequently, our brains are vastly inferior to even a small computer when it comes to reliable storage of data. The brain has no memory units that are stable or can be relied upon not to change. In a computer you can call up file A and be assured that the contents of file A will not change as a result of being recalled. Not so in the brain. If you call up file A in the brain, you will inevitably change it in some way.

Because of these differences in the way transistors and synapses function, computers can take in information only in a one-dimensional way, whereas brains can take in information two-dimensionally. When a picture is presented to a computer, the computer scans it like a television camera. In effect, it takes the two-dimensional picture, cuts it up into slices and swallows them one at a time. The eye, however, can take in the entire two-dimensional picture at one time and transmit the information along the thousands of parallel paths that go to the brain.

The fact that synapses perform the function of processors appears to be a key factor in the way the brain functions. Because each synapse can change its own strength, each one is able to change the circuitry of the brain and influence behavior to some extent. Apparently because of this ability, organisms with nervous systems show adaptive learning; that is, they are able to change their behavior on the basis of their experience.

How do synapses manage to provide the brain with adaptive learning? How do they function as processors and change their own strength? There has been a lot of debate about these changes, and I am now in the middle of it with a theory that attempts to explain the changes and how they cause learning. This is the theory of the "rest principle." (*Psychology Today*, "How the Mind Recharges Batteries," November 1982). It postulates that synapses get weaker when they are overused and that they rapidly get stronger when they are resting after having been used, which enables them to function more effectively.

Here's an example of how the rest principle works. You might be talking to someone and suddenly forget a word. You stop talking and concentrate on trying to remember it. It still doesn't come to mind, so you give up and go on to something else, then suddenly the word flashes into your mind. The reason it happens this way is because by shifting your concentration away from the word, you are giving the synapses engaged in processing the information a rest, and they are able to work better as a result.

Whether synapses really do obey the rest principle is a question for future research. But the principle does work in computers. Making a computer program that produces a specific type of adaptive learning is easy. For instance, to learn the correct response for getting food, the program only needs to keep track of what responses have been successful in the past and then choose the one that has been the most successful. I am sure that with the necessary sensors and means for affecting its environment, a computer programmed to simulate the rest principle would learn to get what it needed from the environment and to escape from things that harmed it. The computer has not yet reached the level of self-preservation that HAL demonstrated in Stanely Kubrick's film *2001: A Space Odyssey*, but it is moving that way.

There are two general approaches for duplicating the actions of synapses in a computer. The first is to simulate them with software. A collection of transistors can be programmed to act like a synapse. The strength of each simulated synapse is recorded in a separate register. When a stimulus is presented to the system, the central processor calculates the path it would probably take through the simulated synapses on the basis of these strengths, and temporal and spatial summation. Then the central processor goes back to each synapse and changes its strength according to the experience it has had, that is, whether the synapse was used or not.

This is the method I have used in simulating the rest principle, and it does work for small systems. It takes, however, a fairly large number of transistors to simulate each synapse, and the central processing unit has to address most of them at least twice for every single event. My simulations have dealt with anywhere from four to 100 synapses. Even on a fast computer, things started going slowly when I got up to 100 synapses. To simulate the 100 trillion or so synapses in the human brain would require a computer with several times this many transistors. If 100 transistors are required to simulate each synapse, a 32-bit processor doing a million operations per second would require several hundred years to address each location once. Several thousand years would be needed to make the calculations for simulating a single event, an event that for humans occupies only a fraction of a second. It seems certain that no matter what advances are made in increasing the speed of computers, they are not going to be able to simulate the human brain on a real-time basis so long as they are restricted to one or even a few dozen processors.

The other approach is to start with basic hardware units that act like synapses. For this we would need components that act like switches but with variable strengths, that are able to process signals in a simple way and that can change their own strengths as a function of experience. The analog computers of the past, which used the decimal system instead of the binary system, had some of these characteristics, and the new analog/hybrid computers of today are much closer to the brain than digital computers are. The analog/hybrid computers use parallel processing (as the brain does), so their speed is relatively independent of the size of the problems. There seems to be no reason why components could not be made that changed their strength as a function of their own experience, for instance, according to the rest principle.

Nevertheless, even if such components were available and 100 trillion of them were connected, you still would not get human-like mental processes. Having such components was only the beginning for living organisms. Evolution has had a long time since then to come up with improvements and modifications. The brain we have today is no homogeneous box of synapses. It is organized into many special structures, and we are only beginning to understand how a few of them are arranged and how they function.

Finally, the brain differs from a computer in that it is immersed in a fluid containing many substances that alter the way the system works. The brain is practically a different machine when certain hormones or modulating substances are floating by it, or when we cause some drug to be dissolved in the solution. Substances diffusing around the brain or in local regions of it seem to form a second means of communication, superimposed on the system of neurons and synapses.

It is unlikely that computers will in the foreseeable future evolve to duplicate the mental functions of even a simple human being. The most useful developments are more likely to come from the interactions and cooperation between these two essentially complementary systems.

Thought

1. List three major differences between the basic units of brains and computers, according to Sinclair. What other important differences exist?
2. Why does Sinclair state that the brain is a better information processor than the computer? Do you agree?
3. How is the brain capable of "adaptive learning"?
4. Paraphrase and evaluate Sinclair's conclusion.

Style and Structure

5. For what purpose does the author declare that he is a biologist?
6. What type of sentence pattern predominates? Why?
7. By referring to the essay, characterize the audience for which "The Hardware of the Brain" was written.

Response and Extension

8. Write two short comparative essays on the relative merits of the brain and computer from the points of view of two of the following:
   a) a computer programmer, b) a chess master, c) a poet, d) a musician, e) an industrialist.
9. Select a place of business and investigate the interaction between human beings and computers. Determine the impact computers have had on that workplace. Present your findings to the class in a report.

The Winter of Man

Loren Eiseley

- What negative connotations do some people associate with winter?

"We fear," remarked an Eskimo shaman responding to a religious question from the explorer Knud Rasmussen some fifty years ago. "We fear the cold and the things we do not understand. But most of all we fear the doings of the heedless ones among ourselves."

Students of the earth's climate have observed that man, in spite of the disappearance of the great continental ice fields, still lives on the steep edge of winter or early spring. The pulsations of these great ice deserts, thousands of feet thick and capable of overflowing mountains and valleys, have characterized the nature of the world since man, in his thinking and speaking phase, arose. The ice which has left the marks of its passing upon the landscape of the Northern Hemisphere has also accounted, in its long, slow advances and retreats, for movements, migrations and extinctions throughout the plant and animal kingdoms.

Though man is originally tropical in his origins, the ice has played a great role in his unwritten history. At times it has constricted his movements, affecting the genetic selection that has created him. Again, ice has established conditions in which man has had to exert all his ingenuity in order to survive. By contrast, there have been other times when the ice has withdrawn farther than today and then, like a kind of sleepy dragon, has crept forth to harry man once more. For something like a million years this strange and alternating contest has continued between man and the ice.

When the dragon withdrew again some fifteen or twenty thousand years ago, man was on the verge of literacy. He already possessed great art, as the paintings in the Lascaux cavern reveal. It was an art devoted to the unseen, to the powers that control the movement of game and the magic that drives the hunter's shaft to its target. Without such magic man felt weak and helpless against the vagaries of nature. It was his first attempt at technology, at control of nature by dominating the luck element, the principle of uncertainty in the universe.

A few millennia further on in time man had forgotten the doorway of snow through which he had emerged. He would only rediscover the traces of the ice age in the nineteenth century by means of the new science of geology. At first he would not believe his own history or the reality of the hidden ice dragon, even though Greenland and the polar world today lie shrouded beneath that same ice. He would not see that what the Eskimo said to Rasmussen was a belated modern enactment of an age-old drama in which we, too, had once participated. "We fear," the Eskimo sage had said in essence, "we fear the ice and cold. We fear nature which we do not understand and which provides us with food or brings famine."

Man, achieving literacy on the far Mediterranean shores in an instant of golden sunlight would take the world as it was, to be forever. He would explore the intricacies of thought and wisdom in Athens. He would dream the first dreams of science and record them upon scrolls of parchment. Twenty-five centuries later those dreams would culminate in vast agricultural projects, green revolutions, power pouring through great pipelines, or electric energy surging across continents. Voices would speak into the distances of space. Huge jet transports would hurtle through the skies. Radio telescopes would listen to cosmic whispers from beyond our galaxy. Enormous concentrations of people would gather and be fed in towering metropolises. Few would remember the Greek word *hubris*, the term for overweening pride, that pride which eventually causes some unseen balance to swing in the opposite direction.

Today the ice at the poles lies quiet. There have been times in the past when it has maintained that passivity scores of thousands of years— times longer, in fact, than the endurance of the whole of urban civilization since its first incipient beginnings no more than seven thousand years ago. The temperature gradient from the poles to the equator is still steeper than throughout much of the unglaciated periods of the past. The doorway through which man has come is just tentatively closing behind him.

So complex is the problem of the glacial rhythms that no living scientist can say with surety the ice will not return. If it does the swarming millions who now populate the planet may mostly perish in misery and darkness, inexorably pushed from their own lands to be rejected in desperation by their neighbors. Like the devouring locust swarms that gather in favorable summers, man may have some of that same light-winged ephemeral quality about him. One senses it occasionally in those places where the dropped, transported boulders of the ice fields still hint of formidable powers lurking somewhere behind the face of present nature.

These fractured mementoes of devastating cold need to be contemplated for another reason than themselves. They constitute exteriorly what may be contemplated interiorly. They contain a veiled warning, perhaps the greatest symbolic warning man has ever received from nature. The giant fragments whisper, in the words of Einstein, that "nature does not always play the same game." Nature is devious in spite of what we have learned of her. The greatest scholars have always sensed this. "She will tell you a direct lie if she can," Charles Darwin once warned a sympathetic listener. Even Darwin, however, alert as he was to vestigial traces of former evolutionary structures in our bodies, was not in a position to foresee the kind of strange mental archaeology by which Sigmund Freud would probe the depths of the human mind. Today we are aware of the latent and shadowy powers contained in the subconscious: the alternating winter and sunlight of the human soul.

Has the earth's glacial winter, for all our mastery of science, surely subsided? No, the geologist would answer. We merely stand in a transitory spot of sunshine that takes on the illusion of permanence only because the human generations are short.

Has the wintry bleakness in the troubled heart of humanity at least equally retreated?—that aspect of man referred to when the Eskimo, adorned with amulets to ward off evil, reiterated: "Most of all we fear the secret misdoings of the heedless ones among ourselves."

No, the social scientist would have to answer, the winter of man has not departed. The Eskimo standing in the snow, when questioned about his beliefs, said: "We do not believe. We only fear. We fear those things which are about us and of which we have no sure knowledge . . . ."

But surely we can counter that this old man was an ignorant remnant of the Ice Age, fearful of a nature he did not understand. Today we have science; we do not fear the Eskimo's malevolent ghosts. We do not wear amulets to ward off evil spirits. We have pierced to the far rim of the universe. We roam mentally through light-years of time.

Yes, this could be admitted, but we also fear. We fear more deeply than the old man in the snow. It comes to us, if we are honest, that perhaps nothing has changed the grip of winter in our hearts, that winter before which we cringed amidst the ice long ages ago.

For what is it that we do? We fear. We do not fear ghosts but we fear the ghost of ourselves. We have come now, in this time, to fear the water we drink, the air we breathe, the insecticides that are dusted over our giant fruits. Because of the substances we have poured into our contaminated rivers, we fear the food that comes to us from the sea. There are also those who tell us that by our own heedless acts the sea is dying.

We fear the awesome powers we have lifted out of nature and cannot return to her. We fear the weapons we have made, the hatreds we have engendered. We fear the crush of fanatic people to whom we readily sell these weapons. We fear for the value of the money in our pockets that stands symbolically for food and shelter. We fear the growing power of the state to take all these things from us. We fear to walk in our streets at evening. We have come to fear even our scientists and their gifts.

We fear, in short, as that self-sufficient Eskimo of the long night had never feared. Our minds, if not our clothes, are hung with invisible amulets: nostrums changed each year for our bodies whether it be chlorophyll toothpaste, the signs of astrology, or cold cures that do not cure: witchcraft nostrums for our society as it fractures into contending multitudes all crying for liberation without responsibility.

We fear, and never in this century will we cease to fear. We fear the end of man as that old shaman in the snow had never had cause to fear it. There is a winter still about us—the winter of man that has followed him relentlessly from the caverns and the ice. The old Eskimo spoke well. It is the winter of the heedless ones. We are in the winter. We have never left its breath.

Thought

1. What significance does Eiseley attach to the paintings in the Lascaux cavern?
2. What does Eiseley present as evidence of the *"hubris"* of modern humanity?
3. Explain the relationship between the "mementoes of devastating cold" and "the alternating winter and sunlight of the human soul."
4. Why does Eiseley assert, "We fear more deeply than the old man in the snow"?

Style and Structure

5. Explain how Eiseley uses winter as a metaphor.
6. How does Eiseley use the words of the Eskimo shaman as a structural device for explaining his thesis?
7. How does Eiseley structure the sentences in the third last paragraph? Why does he do this?

Response and Extension

8. Discuss the possible effects upon human life of a new ice age. Write a short story about a future ice age.
9. Write an explanatory essay which examines one of the ways in which humankind could alter radically the climate of the earth, e.g., "nuclear winter," "the greenhouse effect."
10. Debate the following statement: "most of all we fear the doings of the heedless ones among ourselves."

Our Native Tongue

Peter Sypnowich

- Who decides what a word means?
- Who decides how a word is to be spelled?
- Who *should* decide how a word is to be spelled?

Hopefully, anyone reading this sentence who is irked by the word *hopefully*—there at the beginning—will instantly concede me the privilege of using it. Not just because *hopefully* 'it is hoped' has been in the *Oxford* dictionary for two editions now, but because an Englishman's right to speak as he pleases, surely the inheritance of Canadians no less than Americans, of the unlettered as well as the literate, is an ancient privilege and a productive one, so productive that it might be said to constitute the genius of our language. The legendary advances of Middle English were made by the common people at a time when the educated were using French, the language of the Norman conquerors. In their daily speech they abandoned some basic rules of Old English grammar, giving us our wonderfully simple adjectives, with no inflectional endings, and our natural, gender-free nouns. Over the next five or six centuries, the people of Britain enriched English with French and Latin, building a triple vocabulary (as with *rise, mount,* and *ascend*). They invented new words like *banter* and *sham*. They made so many changes that, in 1712, Jonathan Swift proposed that an English academy be established to fix all usage. His proposal was rejected as contrary to the spirit of English liberty; Samuel Johnson, though sympathetic, said many Englishmen would be willing to disobey the edicts of an academy, and some would be proud to do so. This tradition of freedom was still alive in the early years of this century when the Society for Pure English was born in the library of the poet Robert Bridges; the committee agreed with Bridges that its tracts would only propose reforms, not decree them, for as Bridges said, "Language is or should be democratic."

Is democracy, in this context, a large word for a small matter? We all cast votes when we choose to say *hopefully, one hopes, I hope, it is hoped, it is to be hoped*, or none of these. But are we interested in the debate?

The rationale for *hopefully* is that people have never taken to the indefinite pronoun *one* ("one hopes"), feeling it to be stilted, and, though they don't want to come right out and say "I hope," they are looking for something more direct than "it is hoped." The common criticism is that *hopefully* is a dangler, an unattached adverb, unless it is used to modify a verb, as in "She looked at him hopefully." The reply is that *hopefully* can modify a sentence, just like *luckily* or *happily* or a dozen other adverbs ("Happily, adverbs have several uses"). This brings further criticism: as sentence adverbs, *happily* and *luckily* mean "with a happy result" and "it is lucky that," but *hopefully* cannot mean "with a hopeful result" or "it is hopeful that." Which in turn brings a further rebuttal: that *hopefully* is no more different from *happily* than *hopeful sign* is from *happy ending*. More can be written about *hopefully* and no doubt has been, but do people really care? Are they concerned about *hopefully* and *prestigious* and *finalize* and all the other burning issues in contemporary language?

The answer, it seems, is yes. In recent years, language manuals have been coming out like diet books. We used to consult yellowed old copies of Fowler's *Modern English Usage*; now we have language authorities like William Safire addressing us in the daily papers. Part of the public interest in English usage might be put down to the Great Reaction, the return to standards from the indulgences of the 1960s. The middle classes, it seems, are once again looking for instruction. Perhaps they are also turning to language in the hope that here at least is one thing that doesn't change. If so, they've gone to the right people. The language pundits are eager to school us all against any attempt to bend the language to say what we mean. It may be too late for them to stop *contacted*, but there is still time to outlaw *chaired* and *hosted*, to put an end to *parenting* and *pressured*. Their sense of purpose was expressed by Dwight Macdonald, a member of the usage panel of the *American Heritage Dictionary*, when he was asked for his opinion of *enthuse*: "By God, let's hold the line on this one!"

In language matters, we are all conservatives. We get nervous—at least I do—when *access*, familiar as a noun, is used as a verb—a verb that apparently can mean either "to gain access to" or "to make accessible." When words don't have the same meaning for everyone, what happens to the currency of English? If there's one thing in contemporary language that's disagreeable to me, it's the inflation by which *effect* becomes *impact* and *plan* becomes *scenario*, accompanied by the devaluation of *anticipate* to "expect" and *transpire* to "happen."

Yet language changes. At heart we know this. We've all been told about this or that word which used to have an entirely different meaning—*shambles*, say, which used to refer to a scene of carnage, or *preposterous*, which used to mean back-to-front. The process of change is going on all the time. Right now, *gender*, of limited use as a grammatical term, is establishing itself as a replacement for *sex*, whose meaning has become increasingly tumescent. The precision of *gender* is evident in a recent *Globe and Mail* title for an article by Mavor Moore: "Music and gender; is there a relationship?" Try using *sex* there.

Such changes are tenaciously resisted by the language reactionaries. That *gender* 'sex' should appear in a *Globe* headline is an indication of how new it is—the paper hasn't got around to banning it yet. *Globe* reporters are issued a stylebook that governs all their usage, prepared, as such books usually are, by an old hand on the paper. In Canada, our only usage authorities seem to be newspapermen who have taken up the English language as a retirement activity. Defending the purity of English is a leisurely pursuit, for a new word or a new meaning requires attention only when significant numbers of people are using it—that is, when its usefulness is proved. As the *Globe* stylebook says in one of its usage notes, "The controversy about *hopefully* has been going on for a dozen years and its use seems to be still increasing. But this is no time to give up the fight."

I've written a stylebook myself, and I know what's involved here. I think I once presumed to give a fashion editor instruction in the proper use of *flair*, something to the effect that it didn't mean style but a nose for style, from Old French *flair* 'to smell'—mercifully, my memory is as hazy as the distinction.

What's involved here is a vested interest. The niceties of English usage are not easily mastered; once mastered, they are not easily given up. This is understandable, if you think about it. Let us suppose there was a time when you started to use *hopefully* at the beginning of sentences, but you were embarrassed to find in *The Careful Writer* by Theodore Bernstein that this was a "solecistic use," and so (after sneaking a look at *solecistic* in the dictionary) you purged it from your vocabulary. For fifteen years you shunned it. You corrected other people. Then you find in *Dos, Don'ts & Maybes of English Usage*—or more likely someone else reads it and informs you of it—that Bernstein has changed his mind, that he now considers the fight against *hopefully* a lost cause. A *lost cause*? Never.

The pedants are not without their uses. We can be grateful to them for helping us resist the temptation to use *Frankenstein* for the monster, to remind us that *infer* is not *imply*, to teach us that *cohort* is not *colleague* or *accomplice.* But practised as they are in distinctions, the reactionaries seem unable to see the difference between error—carelessness or ignorance or even pretension—and the social and perceptual changes that lead to new words, or new meanings for old ones. For instance, they would not say, as you or I would, that they've had "a hectic day." Though *hectic* is defined in the *Gage Canadian Dictionary* as "filled with or characterized by great excitement or confusion," the pedants find its meaning at some point on the road back to its origins in the Greek *hexis* 'habit.' They have discovered that *hexis* became *hektikos* 'habitual, consumptive,' moved through Latin and Old French into Middle English as *hecktick* in the sense of "hectic fever," and in the seventeenth century came into use as "feverish." And so they stand foursquare with Henry Fowler, who in 1926 wrote triumphantly, "A hectic flush is one that is accounted for not, like other flushes, by exceptional and temporary vigour of emotion but by the *habit* (Greek *hexis*) *of body* called consumption."

In their struggle against "ignorant, obfuscatory change, unnecessary change," as John Simon calls it, the pedants see themselves as defenders of meaning. Why, they ask, should *aggravate* 'make worse' be sacrificed to people who use it in place of perfectly good words like *annoy, irritate* and *exasperate?* But it is not that simple.

There are words whose meanings it would be desirable to abandon, for they are perverse: *presently*, meaning "shortly," not "at present," and *fulsome*, meaning "excessive," not "abundant"; in usage both of these words are now assuming their logical meanings, which they originally possessed.

In another category are words whose old meanings, though useful, are certainly not as valuable as their new ones. *Anachronism* meaning "a thing outdated" has ruled out the literary term meaning "error in chronology," for such an error is invariably ahead of its time, not outdated— in the film *Chariots of Fire*, for example, the maple leaf that appears on the singlet of a Canadian runner at the 1924 Olympics. We might miss the old meaning of *anachronism*, but who would want to sacrifice the convenience of calling it an anachronism?

In yet another category are words whose meanings are not necessarily destroyed by their new ones. *Disinterest*, a neater, more emphatic way of saying "lack of interest," does not necessarily rule out *disinterested* 'impartial.' *Evacuate* is still "to empty," as in "The town was evacuated," although "to remove" now seems more useful, as in "Fifty thousand people were evacuated."

Finally, there are words like *meticulous* which represent distinct losses. It is regrettable, but the original, pejorative meaning of *meticulous*—

'excessively careful'—can no longer be sustained. The word is now used to mean simply "extremely careful"; these days it seems you can't be too careful. Of course, there are those who studiously avoid the new meaning. One would like to call them meticulous.

Who decides what a word means? The people who use it, or the pedants? For two or three hundred years the pedants have been fighting *aggravate* 'annoy,' but it won't go away. People find it useful. As a doublet of *aggrieve*, influenced by *aggression*, it carries the idea of blame; someone who is "aggravated" remains a good fellow, whereas if he is "annoyed" or "irritated" or "exasperated" he may be just cranky. *Aggravate* 'annoy' and *aggravate* 'make worse' easily coexist because one applies to people and the other does not. Those of us who don't like it can make a point of using *aggravate* as often as possible to mean "exacerbate." What we can't do, any more than the pedants of the last two centuries, is ban *aggravate* 'annoy' from the King's English. It is in the vocabulary of the future king himself; he used it in a speech during his visit to the Maritimes in 1983.

In the end, usage prevails. It may have taken the better part of sixty years for people to accept *finalize*, which the Australians introduced to the language, patterning it on *baptize* and *notarize*, but now we have a swarm of similar derivatives. New language may seem queer, and we may look down our noses at those who use it, but if a word or meaning is useful it will survive, and the pedants should accept it with grace if not gratitude.

I remember flinching at *finalize* in university. The word was used at a student council meeting where I was censured for "poor taste" in publishing in the *Ubyssey* the names of fraternities that excluded Jews and non-whites. It was my high school rival who said, "I move we finalize the motion." After that, *vandalize, internalize, hospitalize* and even *sensitize* were easy to swallow (but not, I confess, *conscientize*).

I mention my encounter with *finalize* because not long ago we all experienced something like it in the Watergate scandal. The villains in the piece used *misspoke* and *inoperative* and other, unliterary language which increased our outrage. For the language pundits, however, the vocabulary of the conspirators had a larger meaning—the decline of English, the end of civilization as we know it. In this they took their cue from George Orwell, who, in his essay "Politics and the English Language," saw a connection between tyranny and big words. Marxists, Orwell noted, used a lot of words translated from foreign languages.

George Orwell wanted to discourage the idea that language is a natural growth rather than, as he put it, "an instrument which we shape for our own purposes." It is true, unfortunately, that people try to shape language for their own purposes. Nationalists, for example, have been at work on English ever since the settlement of the New World. In England they halted the conversion of *-our* endings to the *-or* spelling, for the latter was seen as an American corruption. Henry Fowler declared that American and British English should not be mixed, an injunction that must leave Canadians speechless.

A more recent political intervention has been that of feminists who, secure in a moral position, have sought to purge English of what they perceive to be male chauvinism. Besides suppressing words like *mankind*, they have insisted on the suffix *-person* for indefinite references and the suffix *-woman* for females. In doing so they interfered with a development in the language that was already under way. The *-woman* suffix collided with a trend away from all expressions of gender, one manifestation being the gradual elimination of words like *authoress* and *aviatrix*. And the arrival of *-person* served to reverse what had been a growing sense of the unstressed *-man* as an indefinite reference, as in *ombudsman* and *chairman*. These regressions are not necessarily going to be offset by the use of *-person*, which is unlikely to survive because in words like *alderperson* and *bogeyperson* it is clumsy. The net effect may be the opposite of what the feminists intended.

The moral approach to English was recently recommended by Geoffrey Nunberg, the linguist who supervised the usage notes in *American Heritage*. He cited the word *lifestyle*. People do have different styles of life, he conceded, but *lifestyle* bothered him: "In giving a one-word meaning to a category we make it into a primary concept, which is presumed to have a basic place in our overall scheme of things." On that basis, we would ban such compound words as *defenestrate* and *kneecap* for fear their ugly meanings would have a basic place in our overall scheme of things. It is true that to write in terms of lifestyle may be to ignore certain moral questions, as do, say, food writers and pornographers. But not even the opponents of pornography would go so far as to call its one-word meanings immoral, even those with only four letters.

If the language pundits don't foresee moral or political collapse, they sense something worse: the decline of English itself. The titles of their works convey an impression that the barbarians are at the gates (*Strictly Speaking: Will America Be the Death of English?* by Edwin Newman) or that they have already overrun us (*The Underground Grammarian*, by Richard Mitchell). But is it true today, any more than in the time of Dean Swift, that English is going the way of the Roman Empire? The spread of education and the growth of publishing would seem to point to something else—a degree of literacy never before attained in English.

True, we've had two or three generations of "sight reading" in the schools, which produced not only pupils but teachers who couldn't spell.

After that we had a permissive approach to learning that tried to persuade us spelling didn't matter. At the same time, linguists were telling us that all usage is valid, that there's no good English or bad English, just current English and obsolete English, and in support of this *Webster's New Third International* appeared without "colloq." beside any of its entries, not even *ain't*.

If all of this was cause for alarm, it no longer is. The schools are back to basics. The linguists are in confusion if not retreat, fretting about phonemes and morphemes. "Colloq." is once again in Webster's. On top of which we have all these books by language authorities, along with a new corrective: stylebooks.

At last count there were 231 stylebooks in English. They are a relatively new phenomenon. *Hart's Rules* for compositors was compiled in England in 1893; the *Chicago Manual of Style* followed in 1906. Stylebooks came into use to ensure consistency in typographical matters such as capitalization and italicization; the new edition of *Chicago* runs to 738 pages and tells you which letters in Finnish get umlauts. Along the way, stylebooks moved into other areas, such as spelling distinctions: *gibe* (insult) and *jibe* (accord), *gauntlet* (glove) and *gantlet* (ordeal). With the multiplication of stylebooks and the copy editors who use them, English is undergoing a refinement and consolidation unmatched since the standardization of spelling and grammar in the seventeenth and eighteenth centuries.

Most people, however, have probably never seen a stylebook. They might wonder about the effects on what is, after all, their language. They have reason to wonder. First, the stylebooks are not in fact consistent. Commercial considerations have intruded into capitalization, so that the typical newspaper stylebook will call for *ferris wheel* but *Frisbee* and *Aspirin, transatlantic* or *pan-Slavic* but *TransCanada Pipelines, the Bible* or *the Titanic* but *The Times* and *The Bay*. These proliferating conceits run counter to what had been steady progress away from the cluttered capitalized texts of the eighteenth century. After all, we don't speak in capital letters.

Second, the stylebooks are closed books. They are written by editors, not writers. The language has always been shaped by those who use it. Today, if you write for publication your opinion on matters of style won't count for anything, except perhaps at the University of Chicago Press, whose style manual is one of the few—perhaps the only one—to make explicit provision for the preference of authors. Elsewhere, a writer who happens to be a socialist will find himself paying tribute to the Johnson & Johnson corporation with capital letters for *Band-Aid solution*, an English purist will find two French accents on *resumé*, or an atheist will find his reference to God followed by a capitalized *He*.

Third, and most important, the stylebooks are not restricted to style. They cover disputed points of grammar and diction. And they get their opinions from—where else?—the language pundits. The *Globe and Mail* stylebook, for instance, contains all the familiar invective—this word is "an abomination," that one is "execrable." The Watergate tapes showed "the appalling depths to which English has fallen." One *Globe* usage note says *shambles* means a slaughterhouse, to be used "only if the blood is really flying." Another says, "Hectic means habitual, not frantic, frenzied or ebullient."

The *Toronto Star* stylebook says of *prestigious*: "The suffix means *full of*, and you can be no more full of prestige than you can be full of reputation; both are absolute words." *Prestigious*, like *lifestyle*, is one of those words the reactionaries love to hate. But contrary to the *Star* stylebook, *prestige* is not "absolute"—you can have more or less prestige. According to *Urdang's Suffixes*, *-ous* means not only "full of" but "characteristic of." Where on earth did the *Star*'s opinion come from? Wilson Follett in *Modern American Usage*: "The word *prestige*, like *reputation*, is an absolute rather than a quantitative term, and just as we do not say *He is full of reputation*, so we ought to find it awkward to say *He is full of prestige*."

Such hand-me-down rulings are not only old (the *Star* stylebook was published eighteen years after Follett's book). They also tend to have a long life. The Canadian Press stylebook, used since 1940 in newspaper offices across the country, developed a list of banned words that by the 1978 edition numbered about fifty; among the forbidden words were the verbs *airlift, contact, deactivate, envision, finalize* and *pressure*. There's a new edition of the CP stylebook in which the ban on those fifty words seems to have been lifted, but you can be sure they will be slow to find their way into Canadian newspapers, having been expunged from the working vocabularies of two generations of journalists. Meanwhile, the new CP stylebook has ruled out, among other things, *aggravate* 'annoy,' *fulsome* 'abundant, profuse,' *gender* 'sex,' *meticulous* 'extremely careful,' and *presently* 'now.'

The newsroom pedants who write the stylebooks, like their mentors the language pundits, are legitimately employed as the servants of writers. But they seek a higher mission. They set out to serve the language. Then we are likely to get, as we now have, what Robert Bridges called the tyranny of professional authority.

Canadians are peculiarly subject to authority in language matters. The coexistence of "British" English and "American" English in this country would appear to give us a unique freedom of choice, but this is illusory. To begin with, Canadians use words like *store* and *cookie* instead of *shop* and *biscuit* not because, as H.L. Mencken had it, Americans forms won out in competition. From the beginning, English-speaking Canada was settled in large part by Americans; the Loyalists who came here after the War of Independence were British subjects but Americans nonetheless, and they brought their language with them.

In this sense Canada has always been an American country and no doubt always will be. But the British connection that brought the Loyalists here made Canadian nationalism an expression of faith in the British Empire—an empire that Canada might one day lead. The result was an official language that persists to this day and, depending on your outlook, can be downright coercive.

This is most evident in spelling. As Mencken recorded with amusement, an order in council in 1890 required Canadian civil servants to use British spellings. Generations of Canadian schoolchildren, particularly in Ontario and British Columbia, were trained accordingly. British forms acquired a ye-olde-gift-shoppe gentility in spellings like *programme*, mandatory for contributors to *Saturday Night* although *program* was usual in Britain until the nineteenth century and was sanctioned by the King's Printer in Ottawa in 1931.

On the other hand, the "American" *-or* spelling is mandatory in newspaper offices, as laid down by the CP stylebook, so that someone who thinks it an act of disloyalty to write *labor* will find the word so spelled in his letter to the editor. At *Chatelaine* magazine, which uses the *New York Times* stylebook with a few amendments, a reader complaining about a "cosy dialogue" between, say, the editors and American feminists, will find it appearing in her letter as "cozy dialog."

Whether *cosy* versus *cozy* or *program* versus *programme*, the dual spellings in this country do not present a choice—at least not to anyone who writes for publication. For writers in Canada, there is a long list of words they are not permitted to spell.

CP spelling has aroused suspicions that it was adopted for convenience in handling the flow of copy for its big sister in New York, Associated Press. But CP is consistent. It applies its *-or* ending to *Canadian Labour Congress*, as the CLC spells its name, and it also applies its *-re* style to American names, so that we get *Lincoln Centre*.

The CBC, in contrast, sticks to *-our* and other traditional spellings, but in its dependence on the American television networks it uses clips of video tape on which are superimposed U.S. designations like "secretary of labor" and "defense secretary" instead of *defence (c)*.

You can understand the aversion to servility in those who would shun

"American" spellings, and such writers should surely be permitted to assert themselves. Anything is better than aping the Americans.

The trouble with clinging to British spelling is that it invites one of two eventualities, both undesirable. The British will go over to the Americans, as they have done with *jail*, and we will find ourselves alone, looking as foolish as the Australians who still use *gaol*. Or, in the absence of any other governing principle, there will be a reaction to the anglophilia of *programme* and American spelling will make a clean sweep.

In 1972, the Survey of Canadian English polled 14,228 students and parents and found *gray* had become nearly as prevalent as *grey*. But the American form is not superior (even in the United States *grey* is fixed in *grey-hound*). Nor is *cozy*, which collides with *rosy*, nor *disk*, which collides with *discus*. While we might all accept *skeptic*, distinct from *sceptre*, as well as *pajamas, plow* and *sulfur*, I for one would not want to see us adopt *center* and *theater*; it may be futile to expect the Americans to turn their back on Noah Webster and follow our example (though *theatre* is still used by some Americans), but the *-re* ending gives us a more rational stem for such derivatives as *theatrical* and *centrifugal, fibrous* and *calibrate*.

The sensible course for Canadians is to opt for rational, progressive spellings. Few would venture down the rocky road of spelling reform. (*Tho* is an improvement on *though*, but do we then spell *dough* as *do*?) Canadians, however, can advance by choosing from spellings that are already in use in this country. If we put aside outdated nationalist sentiments, we might create a consensus that Canadian spelling is not "British" or "American" but the best.

We might, for instance, uniformly use the British single *l* in such words as *distil* and *instalment* and even *wilful*, an advance resisted by some people in the belief it is American. With this reform we might get *wooly* as well as *woolen, marvelous, tranquilizer* and *jewelry* (plus *jeweler*). In time we might even get the single-*l traveling* to match the single-*r entering*, as well as the single-*p worshiped* to match the single-*t benefited*. In school we were taught to double these consonants to indicate that the preceding vowel is soft, but since only vowels with stress are hardened in English, we can have *traveled* in contrast to both *reviled* and *rebelled*. Though the doubled *l* seems to be mandatory in all Canadian stylebooks, the Survey of Canadian English found twenty-three per cent using *traveled*.

Unlike the Americans, who will both "practice pretense" and "license service," we make an agreeable distinction by reserving *c* for nouns and *s* for verbs. This urge to distinction might prompt us to keep some traditional spellings, such as *storey* and *cheque*. When we finally drop the *u* in words like *cauldron* and *moulding*, we might hang on to *mould* for the parasite and even *moult* in distinction to *molten*.

There's no reason, however, to retain superfluous letters in words of foreign origin. We're likely to move on from *omelet* to *epaulet* and *cigaret*, from *furor* to *mustache*, and we might accelerate our abandonment of diphthongs and get *esthetic, ameba, fetus*, and so on. (One of my personal causes is *maneuvre*, which would retain our *-re* ending but get rid of the *o* frozen in *manoeuvre*.)

The Survey of Canadian English found that *color* had become almost as popular as *colour*, which is perhaps no surprise in view of the difficulties surrounding the *-our* ending. Derivatives, for instance, sometimes drop the *u* (*coloration*) and sometimes keep it (*colourful*). The rule in the *Oxford Guide to the English Language* is that *u* is retained before the suffixes *-able, -er, -ful, -ism, -ist, -ite* and *-less*, but dropped before *-ation, -ize, -ific* and *-ous*. Who can remember all that? Then there is the basic problem of sorting out the like of *vigour* and *torpor*. Most Canadians probably have no idea which words have dropped the *u*. Let us suppose you want to be 100 per cent Canadian, i.e., British. Ask yourself which of the following "British" spellings are incorrect; *ardour, clamour, clangour, misdemeanour, rancour*. Answer: None. Then ask yourself which of the following "American" spellings should have *-our* endings: *pallor, tremor, squalor, stupor*. Answer: None. As Fowler said, there seems to be no discernible line between the two forms. The *Oxford Guide* has tried to draw one by resorting to the expedient of exceptions; it says agent nouns take *-or* (except for *saviour*) and abstract nouns take *-our* (except for *error, horror, languor, liquor, pallor, squalor, stupor, terror, torpor* and *tremor*). But this doesn't cover it. *Author, carburettor, mirror* and *motor* are not agent nouns, and *armour, neighbour, odour* and *vapour* are not very abstract. The burden of mastering these distinctions can't long be sustained as a condition of Canadian citizenship.

All of the rational spellings I've mentioned are in use in this country, but it is a remarkable fact that no writer in the media, or probably government and education, would be permitted to use them all. This demonstrates the effects of nationalism—and the extent to which written language can serve as an instrument of authority.

That Canadian English is a poor vehicle for nationalism is evident in the paucity of purely Canadian words. Those we have contributed to the language are mostly French or Indian and deal with the outdoors, such as *muskeg* and *toboggan*, though *kerosene, totem* and more recently *hotliner* are notable. Those we have retained as peculiarly our own, excluding terms like *separate school*, in which the thing, not the word, is particular, comprise mostly regionalisms like *floathouse* and *hydro*. The list of general words exclusive to Canada runs to not many more than twenty; it includes *freeze-up, landed immigrant, saw-off* and the malformed *endorsation*. (One Canadian word I've never seen in print, not even in the *Dictionary of Canadianisms*, is *cotton batten*, meaning *cotton wool*, presumably a corruption of *cotton batting*). The word most likely to identify you as a Canadian in both Britain and the United States is *chesterfield*, preferred eight-to-one over *sofa* in the Survey of Canadian English; for the British and the Americans, a chesterfield is an overcoat (in Britain it is also, obscurely, a sofa with arms the same height as its back).

The stylebook purists pay little attention to distinctively Canadian words, perhaps because it is beyond their powers to make writers use them. Instead their vigilance is directed at intruders. As with spelling, it is Americanisms that are feared, although there are five times as many British words with no currency in this country. American usage has a special role. It serves as a club. The very first injunction in the *Globe* stylebook is the hoary old rule against *talk with*—you "talk *to*, (not *with*; you confer *with*)." The notion that a writer must use *confer* when he means *talk*, that you can run *with* someone but you can only talk *to* him, is—well, not very interesting. What is interesting is that the *Globe*'s injunction follows a warning against "sloppy American usage." The *Oxford* dictionary, which is about as un-American as you can get, begins its half-a-column on *talk* as follows: "1. v.i. Converse, communicate ideas, by spoken words, (*was talking with* or *to a friend*)."

The list of real Americanisms runs to more than 100, and keeping them all out is a daunting task for the border patrol. The old CP stylebook banned *escalation* and *prestigious* as American, opted for *railway* over railroad and *reserve* over *reservation*, and then said, vaguely but fiercely, "Deskmen should be alert to lop out such Americanisms." The new CP stylebook omits all this, confining itself to a couple of legal injunctions—not *attorney* but *lawyer*, not *witness stand* but *witness box*—and a spit-and-polish note on military terms—not *honor guard* but *guard of honor*, not *boot camp* but *basic military training*. The *Globe* stylebook is no more helpful: "Penny as a designation for a one-cent coin is an Americanism and one which should be shunned by careful writers. But alas the good old Canadian term of copper for the coin has all but vanished."

The arrival of American words in Canada, though sometimes felt acutely, is not necessarily harmful. *Bagman* in the United States is a collector in the numbers racket; it serves us well as the word for a political fundraiser. American words may displace Canadian equivalents, but sometimes they simply coexist with them, giving us—on a much smaller scale—a double vocabulary like that which arose in England after the Norman invasion. Thus we have *crown attorney* for prosecutor and *lawyer* for counsel; we opt for the British *face cloth* and use the American equivalent, *washcloth*, for other purposes.

If the Canadian vocabulary is more ungovernable than Canadian spelling, Canadian speech is a law unto itself. Linguistic field workers report many variations in how we say our words. The differences are not only regional but individual, and they vary even there, so that (as Mark Orkin noted in *Speaking Canadian English*) one person might pronounce *either* as "eether" but *neither* as "nyther." Yet Canadian pronunciation is remarkably homogeneous—certainly more so than either British or American English. In the United States you can tell a southerner by the way he says *greasy*—he rhymes it with *easy*. We have nothing to match that. Nowhere in English-speaking Canada, not even in Newfoundland, perhaps, is there a regional accent as distinct as Dixie speech, Boston speech or New York speech, or anything to match the disparate dialects of Britain (only three per cent of the British speak with the prestigious accent known as Received Pronunciation).

The language we speak is very close to what used to be called General American, a dialect spoken with some variations throughout the mid-western and western United States. About the only really distinct pronunciation in General Canadian is "karky" for *khaki*, which the British rhyme with *cocky* and the Americans with *tacky*. Canadians can be distinguished from Americans by a subtle difference in our pronunciation of diphthongs before unvoiced consonants; some Americans hear it as "oot" for *out* and "aboot" for *about*. Canadians in turn are conscious of such American pronunciations as "lehver" for *lever*, "rowt" for *route* and of course "zee" for *z*. Yet Canadians are steadily abandoning "British" pronunciations, saying, for example, "stoodent" for *student*. In 1970, Mark Orkin averred that *lieutenant* was "always and only a 'leftenant'"; two years later, the Survey of Canadian English showed seventy-five per cent of students said "lootenant." The broad *a* in *tomato*, which I learned at my mother's knee (and still use), is heard nowhere in Canada now, not even on the CBC. I've met utter failure trying to get my four children to avoid "skedule" for *schedule*; along with seventy-five per cent of students in the Survey of Canadian English, they'll have nothing to do with "shedule." As one my daughters said, "Shedule as in shool, eh?"

Canadian pronunciation tends to be rational. We use what is called a spelling pronunciation, meaning that we say it as we write it. Not for us the clipped British pronunciation of "secretry" and "medsin." This makes us slow to follow the general trend in English to shift stress onto first syllables. In a recent hearing of a complaint of sexual harassment, the participants were surprised to hear the CBC television reporter suddenly (on the instructions of her producer) stressing the first syllable in *harassment*. Not one of the participants said it that way.

"The rather lovely sound of the soft Canadian accent" is perhaps not as soft or lovely as it was when Rupert Brooke called it that in 1913. As many Canadians are now saying *butter* as "budder" and *genuine* as "genu-yne." But we still say "rashun" for *ration*, as the British do (the Americans say "ray-shun"), and we still say "missl" for *missile* as the Americans do (the British say "miss-ile"). In its resemblances to both American and British speech, Canadian language enjoys an enviable universality, as our actors and television reporters have found.

Edwin Newman, in the new *NBC Handbook of Pronunciation*, confesses that he spent half his life saying "ahrinj" for *orange*: "It wasn't until a Californian took pity on me...that I learned that the fruit was an OR-inj. After all, I didn't say 'ahr' for 'or,' did I?"

There are two remarkable things about this statement. One is that Newman should think his pronunciation of a vowel incorrect. Although there is usually agreement on whether a vowel should be hardened, its quality is otherwise determined by a speaker's origins. Here, in disdain of the accents of New England and the South, we hear the beginning of a claim for General American that once was heard for Received English. The second interesting thing about Newman's confession is that it was a Californian who corrected him. Californian speech is probably even closer to Canadian than the General American heard immediately south of the forty-ninth parallel, and the pronunciation presented by Newman as "correct" is the pronunciation you would hear almost anywhere in Canada.

Something else is happening, too. "The great Canadian *r*," as it's been called, is now prevailing. The early Canadians, for reasons that are not entirely clear, began to sound the so-called post-vocalic *r* in words like *car* and *fear*, abandoning the British pronunciation—"cah" and "feah"—that had become established in New England and the American South. In an article on American speech in *English As a World Language*, Frederick Cassidy reports that the post-vocalic *r* is being restored by young people in the South and is also gaining in prestige in New York City. Something similar is occurring in Britain, as can be detected by anyone who listens closely to British movies and television.

When we get away from the authority of print, away from the schoolbooks and rule books, away from "Canadian" spelling and "Canadian" vocabulary, we begin to see just how successful our language is becoming. It gives you new respect for freedom of speech.

In his 1951 study of Canadian language for the Massey report, Professor Henry Alexander, head of the English department at Queen's University, shared none of the prevailing anxiety about American culture. He suggested that our schools teach American spelling, since its few reforms had made English spelling at least slightly less illogical and chaotic. What concerned him was the low level of nonprofessional writing in this country, and what he wanted to do about it was to provide instruction in speech—from grade school right through university. "Good speech habits," he said, "will produce good writing."

Few people listened. Then as now, we were losing sight of the connection between written and spoken language. Young littérateurs took bookish pride in the words they'd learned to read but not pronounce. Speech was for salesmen and evangelists; even the politicians were turning to speech writers. The exaltation of literature had petrified English in the form of the Victorian essay, and educated people didn't even hear themselves saying, "It is me."

If English has come to seem a dead language, like Latin, written but not spoken, this is a legacy of the grammarians of the eighteenth and nineteenth centuries—the same men who forbade the split infinitive because in Latin an infinitive consists of one word, who held that a preposition could not end a sentence because in Latin it precedes a noun. The Latin grammarians gave us "colloquial" as a dictionary code word for substandard, and very handy it was, too: on the theory that speech was but a testing ground for print, anything new could simply be given the label "colloq." The *Oxford English Dictionary* definition of *colloquial* quotes Dr. Johnson: "To refine our language to grammatical purity, and to clear it from colloquial barbarisms." (Notice the construction *from*, which in 1752 had been archaic for a century.)

It's perfectly true that some language is slow to enter print, and some may never get in at all. The expressive slang you use with your friends, the convenient jargon you use with your workmates—such language is not for strangers who might not understand it. For the same reason, writers exercise a let-George-do-it caution about using new words or new meanings; even if it's understandable to everyone now, will it still be current in ten or twenty or fifty years? The universal and the enduring are what give the printed word its power.

Nevertheless, written language has always been and always will be a representation of speech. If you don't say it, you can't write it. The rule is always that written language must meet the test of speech, not the other way around.

This rule is often broken by journalists who like to think they use plain language. An example is the practice of using the possessive to indicate place, as in "Toronto's CN Tower." This syntax is alien to speech; no one would ever say it. And succinct as it is, it does not advance the language. When we began abandoning inflections in Middle English, we reserved the *s* genitive for animate nouns as an expression of possession. The arrival of the uninflected adjective permitted us to say "a table leg" rather than "a table's leg." To use the *s* genitive in "Toronto's CN Tower" is a step back to the inflections of Old English.

The limitations of the genitive—indeed, the very idea of case—become apparent in one of the great disputes of English usage. Should we say, "She didn't like him hanging around," or, "She didn't like his hanging around"? Henry Fowler insisted on the genitive, calling the accusative a "fused participle," and I remember seeing Margaret Atwood follow this rule in a business letter to me. The great Otto Jespersen demonstrated that there are many instances in which the genitive is impossible, as in "I don't approve of the young's having the vote." But while it is all right to use "the young" in that sentence, we begin to understand what Fowler meant by the fused participle when we write, "Him hanging around disturbed her." The truth is that case is a nuisance in English. Now that we've pretty well abandoned the nominative after the verb *to be* ("It is me"), and given up the accusative *whom* in questions ("Who did he want?"), we might move on and get rid of case entirely. Someday we might recognize the contribution to English made by the Ape Man when he said, "Me Tarzan."

A solution to another vexing problem is already at hand in our everyday speech. We say, "Everyone wants to have their cake and eat it too." *Everyone* has long been felt as a plural—doesn't it mean "all"?—and so we use the plural pronoun *their*. Yet the logic of *one* tells us it is singular, so we use *wants* in the third person singular. In writing, we resolve this contradiction by using *his* as an indefinite pronoun: "Everyone wants to have his cake." But the masculine pronoun becomes embarrassingly definite in a subsequent clause: "Everyone wants to have his cake, but he wants to eat it too." *He* and *his* as indefinite pronouns run into the aversion to grammatical gender we've had since Middle English. Under the influence of the feminists, we might someday recognize *they* and *their* as indefinite pronouns of indefinite number, and write, "Anyone can choose their own pronouns," or even "A writer can use the pronoun they wants."

English syntax will never be perfect—as the philologist Edward Sapir said, all grammar leaks. But English seems to be suffering from arrested development in its drift to an inflectionless language. Written language may not be entirely responsible for this. But it's the spoken word—ever seeking short cuts, ever shaking off excrescences—that will take us where we're going.

Broadcasting might help to restore the primacy of speech. It is undoubtedly standardizing the Canadian accent. Perhaps it will advance our syntax and our vocabulary. Unfortunately, much of what is said on television and radio is scripted, and many of the writers got their start on newspapers. Knowlton Nash's language is distinctly superior to the journalese of Dan Rather on CBS. But in general broadcasters are as intimidated as anyone else by the language pundits, and there is as much verbicide in the studios as in the newsrooms. CBC Radio News has a stylebook with a list of "not wanted words" which includes *finalize*. The BBC handbook *A Question of Style* rules out *implement* and *campus* and a dozen other words; *hospitalize*, listed in Oxford for three editions, is "dreadful American jargon."

Does the English language, and more particularly the Canadian language, have a future? English is an official language in thirty-seven countries, spoken by 300 million people as a native language and by nearly as many as a second language. Its vocabulary, though enormous (more than 450,000 words), is familiar to many foreigners because of its borrowings from their own languages—and because their languages in turn have had to borrow from English. As the imperial language for more than two centuries, the medium of new products, new social arrangements and new ideas, English has come close to becoming the official world language. When its imperial authority declines, as might be happening now, will English have the perception and energy to create new words like *lifestyle* and rework the meanings of old ones like *hectic*? Or will it be dulled by dependence on the concepts and coinages of another language—say, Chinese, which in its many dialects is already spoken by more people than any other language? There are other challenges. Can English simplify its inconsistent, archaic spelling, which makes it so hard for other people to learn? Will it finally rid itself of case and tense, making itself as simple as Chinese, which freely uses any word as a verb or noun or adjective?

These are challenges for you and me and our children to meet, for if English has a destiny, it is the destiny of Canadian language. By an accident of history and geography, we enjoy the most universal of dialects. We speak English with the accents that will be spoken in the future. If we are going to write the language of the future, we will close our ears to the scratching of quill pens and the cries of the pedants. We will listen to our own voices. Hopefully.

Thought

1. What does Sypnowich mean by the "genius of our language"?
2. What statements best illustrate what happens "when words don't have the same meaning for everyone"?
3. Find several examples which show that "people try to shape language for their own purposes." As a class, discuss several examples from your own experience.
4. Account for the "British" spellings of words in Canadian usage.
5. Sypnowich states that "Canadian English is a poor vehicle for nationalism." Do you agree?
6. Find several examples to show that "all grammar leaks."
7. Do you agree with Sypnowich that Canadians "enjoy the most universal of dialects"? Is this a positive or negative characteristic for a language?

Style and Structure

8. Why does the author begin and end his essay with the word "hopefully"?
9. What does the title of the essay indicate about the author's relationship to his subject? Explain.
10. Suggest ways to condense this essay to one half of its length without disturbing the essence of Sypnowich's explanation.

Response and Extension

11. Debate the following statement: "Language is or should be democratic."
12. Read a book that exploits the way in which Canadians use the English language, for example, *Charlie Farquharson's Histry of Canada* by Donald Harron; *The Rowdyman* and *John and the Missus* by Gordon Pinsent; "Lark Song" by W.P. Kinsella; *Blood Flowers* by W.D. Valgardson. Present a report to your class on the variety of Canadian dialect in that book.

Unit Synthesis

1. Using Syfers' essay as a point of reference, explain the marriage relationships that are portrayed in any two of the following plays: *Macbeth, King Lear, Romeo and Juliet, A Man for All Seasons, Death of a Salesman, A Streetcar Named Desire, Who's Afraid of Virginia Woolf, A Doll's House.*

2. By referring to "The Way of All Flesh," write an essay explaining the portrayal of the aged in a Canadian novel such as *The Stone Angel, Who Has Seen the Wind, A Bird in the House, Fifth Business, The Rowdyman, A Fine and Private Place.*

3. Explain the depiction of "artificial intelligence" in contemporary film and television, for example, *2010 A.D., Star Wars, A Hitch-Hiker's Guide to the Galaxy, War Games,* etc.

4. Read one of Loren Eiseley's collections of essays (*The Immense Journey* or *The Star Thrower*). Select one of the essays from either collection and present a summary of the thoughts within this essay.

5. Write an essay which explains the way computers and computer programming have influenced everyday language.

6. Read "The Unspeakable State of Soliloquy" by William H. Gass (p. 175). Compare and contrast the conclusions of Gass and Sypnowich with respect to the public and private uses of language.

Writing to Analyze a Process

The analysis of a process usually begins with general remarks about the nature of the phenomenon to be investigated. Often a causal relationship is noted. Then the steps of the process are scrupulously examined in the appropriate sequence.

Robert Brody investigates the impact of anger upon athletic performance. "Distracted from the business at hand, my concentration in smithereens, I could usually count on my game to self-destruct."

Because of the attention to concrete detail in process analysis, there is little room for speculation. Process implies action and the author must track this movement in a factual way. "The first tentative electrons probe toward the earth in a series of steps that gives a lightning bolt its irregular shape," writes Janice McEwen. "These first electrons clear a path for those in the cloud, and as soon as the first electrons connect with the ground, an avalanche of electricity surges from the sky."

It is one thing to observe a process and analyze its component parts; it is quite another thing to describe that process in words, as Ted Hughes points out. "It is when we set out to find words for some seemingly quite simple experience that we begin to realize what a huge gap there is between our understanding of what happens around us and inside us, and the words we have at our command to say something about it."

Of the three essayists represented here, Hughes has perhaps taken on the most difficult process to analyze, for he is wrestling with the way in which human beings translate experience into words. Although this process is a very exciting one, it is often frustrating. "It is one thing to get the information, and quite another to become conscious of it, to know that we have got it."

Competing with Cool

Robert Brody

- In small groups, list and discuss the benefits and drawbacks of competitive sport.
- How important is winning?
- Does it feel different to win as a team than it does to win as an individual? Explain.
- How do you cope with losing?
- What is the essence of "cool"?

Even as a kid, I had a talent for getting ticked off in competition. No occasion was too trivial for a tantrum, whether I was striking out, dropping a pass, or blowing a lay-up. In my more-reserved moments I had the decency to blame such failures on myself. But I also had a knack for discerning obscure causes that ranged from lucky curveballs and errant winds to lazy teammates and uncooperative backboards. In retrospect, it was uncanny how seldom I was at fault.

Of course, all my fuming and cursing were bad news when it came to the caliber of my play. The more upset I became at my shortcomings, the worse I performed. I swung at bad pitches, forced jump shots from well beyond my range, double-faulted ad nauseam. Distracted from the business at hand, my concentration in smithereens, I could usually count on my game to self-destruct. In short, I had no cool.

Now that I'm an adult, poise is still not my specialty. Just a few months back, a guy guarding me in basketball was hacking at my arms every time I took a shot and was climbing over my back for rebounds. After one especially nasty foul—I remember feeling to make sure my head was still attached—I shoved him to the court. He laid off me from then on, but no matter—I was so ashamed of my violence that my game was hopelessly undermined for the night.

And so it has gone my whole life. Under competitive pressure I have all the composure of an unfed Doberman. My anger gets so far out of hand that whatever skills I possess are seriously hampered. Only recently have I begun to realize that playing with poise is essential to a top-notch performance in any sport. Poise in this regard means a sense of emotional balance. Just about all the best athletes know that harnessing the emotions can spell the difference between the mediocre and the champion, that staying unruffled in the face of adversity is as much a sign of character as it is an act of sportsmanship.

For the weekend jock as well as the pro, keeping cool in the heat of competition is more often a cultivated skill than an inborn trait. Even if you're the kind of hothead who snaps your 4 iron after a slice into the trees—so bent on excellence that you simply bear down too hard—you can still shed your reputation as a crybaby and salvage your game. Training yourself in techniques for self-control is really no sweat.

The key to keeping your feelings off your sleeve is to try stabilizing the degree to which you become aroused. The prevailing theory is that the simpler the athletic task, the more psyched you should become. For example, intense drive is conducive to producing the explosive strength called for in throwing the shot put, weight lifting, or blocking in football. But you can excel at foul shooting, golf, or archery only if you are calm enough to maintain precision, finesse, and a delicate touch. In other words, you can play well in the service of tension and anxiety— after all, nobody is immune to excitement—as along as you can set your flame at the right temperature for the sport in question.

Burning too hot in competition can lead to anger, an emotion much overrated as an incentive in sports. If you go into conniptions after muffing a ground ball, you're probably draining away energy that you'd be better off conserving for the next play. The infantile rages of John McEnroe serve as proof that a hair-trigger temper is more likely to aggravate hostility than mollify it. "We're always our own worst enemy," says Bruce Ogilvie, a leading sports psychologist and consultant to professional athletes. "Some athletes have only a marginal capacity for adapting to stress, while others cannot function without some tension and anxiety. It's important to find the arousal level appropriate for each of us."

Anger can also be a serious strategic error. By swearing or slamming your tennis racket into a fence after being aced, you're inviting opponents to exploit your deepest vulnerabilities.

My friend David often gets riled during tennis matches—always at his own expense. He tries so hard to win that he swings his racket with unnecessary force, sacrificing accuracy for power. He thus has the distinction of belting the ball into the net or over the base line harder than anyone I know. What David is doing, more or less, is known as choking.

Choking is visible evidence that your body is a slave to your mind—that, more specifically, your emotional state during competition dictates your neuromuscular actions. Let's say you're thinking too much and pushing too hard during a game. You become worried and self-conscious to the point of panic. Your left brain hemisphere shifts into overdrive for the emergency. Your pituitary gland lets loose more adrenaline than your central nervous system can comfortably handle. Nerve impulses give your muscles scrambled instructions.

Now your body starts to conk out. Your heart thumps faster, your pores expand, your pupils dilate, your bronchial tubes tighten, your skin feels clammy. Your breathing is shallow, your mouth dry as sandpaper. Your digestive system shuts down to pump more blood into the muscles and, in so doing, touches off in your stomach the fluttering known as butterflies. Your sense of balance goes askew; your reflexes have no snap. Your jaw, neck, and back muscles knot with tension. Your arms and legs turn stiff and leaden, your movements jerky and uncoordinated.

The upshot is that you've psyched yourself out. You cannot function, concentrate, or make strategy because your judgment has become suspect. You throw to the wrong base, run for a touchdown in the wrong direction.

"Everybody chokes in the clutch," says Gary Krahenbuhl, chairman of the physical education department at Arizona State University. "Some just choke less."

Some athletes are naturally blessed with glacial equanimity. The best display of athletic self-control I ever witnessed took place about eleven years ago in an NBA play-off game. Walt Frazier of the New York Knicks was outclassing his opponent, Phil Chenier of the Baltimore Bullets. At one point, as Frazier was dribbling the ball up the court Chenier felt so stymied that he smacked him on the back of the head. Frazier never so much as flinched, much less cried foul. And, to cap it off, he went one-on-one with Chernier all through the second half, scoring on every shot. Say what you will, that man was *born* cool.

The trick is to make your anger an asset. To an extent, it's really a matter of working the hydraulics of your body chemistry so that your neurotransmitters—the chemical couriers that deliver messages to your cells—behave appropriately. Ideally, exercise physiologists believe, high serotonin levels and low to moderate amounts of dopamine and adrenaline can keep you loose. "In the end," says Bruce Ogilvie, "you have no defense against getting ticked off. The key is how well and how fast you can handle your anger. You just have to program yourself to be in command of your emotions."

You can go far toward protecting yourself against stress in competition if you shoot for sensible objectives. The tennis freak who is obsessive about beating everyone in straight sets, for instance, is not only bucking for disappointment but guaranteeing failure as well. Your next step is to identify what gets you peeved. You can free yourself from anger only after you've pinpointed its causes. Perhaps you sulk because your doubles partner hustles less than you'd like or because your handball adversary cheats. Reflect, if you will, on how you react to such anxieties. Do you ape the misbehavior, in turn hustling less or starting to cheat? Decide now how you'd *like* to adapt to those situations.

Another vital approach to competing with the right bearing is to acknowledge that mistakes are inevitable and educational. Your best bet for capitalizing on mistakes is to figure out exactly what went wrong and, once you've resolved not to repeat it, forget it ever happened. "Assimilate every mistake without dwelling on it," says Dr. Richard M. Suinn, head of the Colorado State University psychology department and psychologist for three 1976 U.S. Winter Olympic teams. "By all means, you should do whatever you can to get off your own back."

Fix your attention on the task you're about to carry out, not on its potential consequences. Think not about whether you're going to sink that eight-foot putt, but about how best to stroke the ball. That way, you'll do yourself the favor of playing with spontaneity. At the same time, try to screen out any peripheral thoughts. "The true champion," says Rainer Martens, physical education professor at the University of Illinois and a U.S. Olympic team consultant, "thinks only about his own performance, not about what his opponents are doing. He also comes to terms with factors he can't control, such as luck and the weather."

Let's assume that however hard you try to practice restraint your frontal lobes still pulse with primal fury during competition. One rather unorthodox technique, if only because it would seem to make you a candidate for a straitjacket, is to talk to yourself. In carrying on a dialogue while you're playing, you can also be your own coach. You can, in effect, keep yourself in perspective, almost as if viewing yourself from outside. You can give yourself technical advice and pep talks, as Billie Jean King and Jimmy Connors frequently do. Derek Harper, now playing with the Dallas Mavericks in the NBA, improved his field-goal shooting percentage by 30 percent in college after experimenting with "selftalk." All you have to do is turn your negative thoughts into positive ones.

A more conventional method for keeping your emotions in check is visualization—playing out in advance a mental scenario of how you'd like to perform. Picture yourself being as unflappable as Bjorn Borg in a

Wimbledon tie breaker. The next time you're tempted to bellyache at being called for a foot fault, the odds are exponentially better that you'll take the decision in stride. You'll be programmed to behave like a gentleman.

Progressive muscle relaxation is also good therapy for anxiety. Take a minute between innings or sets to tense each of your major muscles for five seconds, then relax, going in sequence from neck, shoulders, and arms to chest, abdomen, and legs. Thus stretched, your muscles cannot help but be more limber, putting you more at ease. This reaction is purely electrochemical—the squeezing out of calcium from your muscle fiber.

Perhaps your best safeguard is breathing regularly at all times, says Dan Landers, physical education professor at Arizona State University. He advises that you breathe evenly and deeply, though not too deeply, lest you hyperventilate and become light-headed. Do so through your diaphragm, not your chest. Such steady breathing helps pump fresh oxygen into the blood cells and body tissues for the manufacture of energy and relays shipments of revitalized blood to the brain. Arthur Ashe overcame his reputation as a "choke" in big matches after mastering breath control.

Once you find out which technique—or which combination—works best for you, you'll be prepared at last to liberate your performance potential. My last tip is this: It's perfectly okay to get angry in competition as long as you can channel your anger in the right direction.

This I discovered in a recent two-on-two basketball game. The guy I was covering drove for the basket, jumped straight into me, and clipped me in the jaw with his outstretched elbow, scoring on the shot. You can bet I was not tickled by this raw aggression. But to call an offensive foul in schoolyard basketball is to risk being branded a candy-ass. Besides, I decided retribution would be infinitely more rewarding. So I went into a fever of concentration. The next time he dribbled the ball toward me, I lunged forward, as if going for a steal. He was faked out by the move, forced to stop dribbling and clutch the ball. Then I pulled off a trick I had never done in twenty-three years of playing basketball. Like a pickpocket, I simply plucked the ball from his hands and scored on a lay-up. The guy was so flabbergasted that he quit the game and left the court with hardly a word. I guess he had no cool.

Thought

1. Trace the steps in the author's analysis of the ways in which anger affects athletic performance.
2. Select those sentences from the essay which state purely practical advice. Do you think this advice is sound? Explain. What portions of the advice do not apply to you? Why not?

Style and Structure

3. Provide several examples from the essay which prove that the author is writing for a specific audience rather than the general reader. Identify that audience.
4. Compile a list of informal expressions used in the essay, e.g., "choking," "ticked off." Provide equivalents for them in formal English usage.
5. Why does the author use so many informal expressions?
6. List all of the sports alluded to in the essay. What is the advantage of mentioning a variety of sports instead of addressing just one?
7. Assess the effectiveness of the author's use of anecdote.

Response and Extension

8. Compile a list of athletic expressions used in everyday discourse, e.g., "you struck out," "I fumbled it." What does the abundance of athletic expressions in the language reveal about our society? Prepare and deliver a short speech to your class on this subject.
9. Write a short story which narrates an incident in which you performed "with cool." Include clear and concrete details in the analysis of your performance.

Thunderstrokes and Firebolts

Janice McEwen

- Recount a personal experience involving lightning.
- In groups, list all of the facts you know about lightning.

Imagine the chagrin of a Renfrew, Ontario farmer who pulled on the handle of a recently repaired barn door one morning following a thunderstorm only to have the door crumble into a heap of individual boards at his feet.

The man was left sheepishly wondering about his carpentry skills until a local lightning protection contractor examined the door and explained that, unknown to the farmer, a bolt of lightning had hit the barn during the storm. Leapfrogging from nail-to-nail along the Z-shaped bracing boards that supported the door, the lightning made its way to the ground. In the process the heat produced by the bolt reduced the nails to dust.

For the 118 passengers aboard an Air Canada DC-8 jetliner, lightning had much more serious consequences: the ill-fated plane crashed in a swampy field shortly after take-off from Montreal in November, 1963. When investigators finished sifting through the rubble of what is still Canada's worst airplane disaster, lightning was high on the list of probable causes.

Lightning is the most awesome of nature's weather phenomena—a single stroke of lightning produces more electricity than the combined output of all electrical power plants in the United States. The average cloud-to-ground lightning bolt averages only six inches in diameter, but attains a core temperature of about 50,000 degrees Fahrenheit—five times the temperature at the surface of the sun.

Each day some 44,000 thunderstorms break out around the globe, the greatest concentration of them within the belt extending 30 degrees north and south of the equator. As you read this there are 1,800 electrical storms raging throughout the world, and by the time you finish this sentence, lightning will have struck earth 100 times.

Too frequently, lightning strikes spell disaster. Each year several hundred North Americans are killed by lightning, and others die in the fires that follow in the wake of electrical storms. Ten thousand forest fires and more than 30,000 building blazes are caused by lightning. Damages to property and loss of timber are estimated at more than 50 million dollars annually.

Yet the scientific study of lightning is still in pioneering stages, leaving unexplained many aspects of the complicated series of events that take place in the five thousandths of a second required for the average lightning bolt to strike.

Scientists are, for example, at a loss to explain "ball" lightning, a rare occurrence in which an orb about 20 centimetres in diameter forms at the lightning impact point. This blinding ball of energy is able to move around at a speed of several metres per second and is said to be accompanied by a hissing sound. Ball lightning is able to pass through closed windowpanes and often disappears with an explosion.

Little wonder that this astounding natural force has always aroused man's curiosity and fear.

For our ancient forefathers, there was no doubt about what caused lightning: various gods were flamboyantly expressing their disapproval of somebody's actions.

Zeus, as legend would have it, was particularly keen to use a handy supply of lightning bolts to express his frequent outbursts of rage. Unfortunate were the troops that attacked friends of this surly deity— Zeus would often step in when his side was losing and tip the tides of battle with a few well-placed bolts among the enemy ranks.

But recent findings by Nobel Prize winner Dr. Harold Urey suggest that the ancients may not have underestimated the nearly divine role lightning plays in terrestrial life.

Through laboratory reconstruction of the atmosphere of the young, lifeless earth—an atmosphere composed of ammonia, methane, hydrogen and water—students of Urey found that when electrical sparks, much like lightning, were passed through this medium, amino acids were created—the first building blocks in the evolution of life.

Recent findings also suggest that we can thank lightning (at least partially) for giving the world plants. Although nitrogen makes up 80 per cent of the earth's atmosphere, in its pure state it is useless to plants.

It has been found that lightning causes atmospheric nitrogen to combine with oxygen, forming nitric-oxide gas. This gas dissolves in rain and falls to the earth as usable nitrates. Some scientists estimate that hundreds of millions of tons of these nitrates are produced by lightning each year. It's enough to make a purveyor of bagged 20-20-20 weep.

Benjamin Franklin, that portly Renaissance man of the eighteenth century, made the first real breakthrough in man's understanding of lightning by determining that it was, indeed, a huge electrical spark. But it is ironic (in light of his factual discoveries) that one of the most prevalent schoolboy myths still surrounding lightning features Mr. Franklin as its main character.

Everyone has heard about Franklin's kite flying antics. What few people realize is that his kite was never struck by lightning. Had it been, either the string would have burned and Mr. Franklin would have lost his kite, or the experimenter himself would have been struck, and the world would have lost an able scholar and statesman.

What happened during this famous flight was that there was enough difference in the electrical charge between the earth and the air at the level of the kite to create a small finger-tingling flow of electrical current through Mr. Franklin's string.

Today we know that conditions leading to electrical storms begin when a strong negative charge builds in rain (cumulo-nimbus) clouds. How this charge develops is still a matter of scientific debate, but an accepted theory is that air turbulence in the clouds creates a build-up of negatively-charged electrons.

Free electrons on the earth directly below the cloud are repelled by the huge numbers of electrons above, and therefore the charge of the earth becomes more positive.

Because opposing charges are attracted to each other, the electrons in the cloud yearn to get to the positive earth.

Air, however, is a poor conductor of electricity. As the cloud matures, the charge continues to build until pressure becomes great enough to permit the electrons to leap through the insulative layer of air.

The first tentative electrons probe toward the earth in a series of steps that gives a lightning bolt its irregular shape. These first electrons clear a path for those in the cloud, and as soon as the first electrons connect with the ground, an avalanche of electricity surges from the sky.

Lightning has struck.

Lightning bolts range from 1,000 to 9,000 feet long, and can attain speeds over 60,000 miles per second.

A lightning bolt seeks the route offering the least electrical resistance in its journey from cloud to ground. Almost any solid object offers an easier path for electricity than air: it could be a tree, a utility pole, a high patch of ground; it could also be your barn, one of your outbuildings—or your house.

Lightning is a hazard deserving special attention from rural dwellers. Grim statistics show that nine out of ten lightning-caused deaths occur outside city limits. Fire authorities estimate that lightning causes up to 37 per cent of all rural building fires.

G.A. Pelletier, chief of technical services in the Ontario Fire Marshall's Office and one of Canada's foremost authorities on lightning, attributes part of this phenomenal loss of life and property in rural areas to people being misinformed about this frightening natural force.

"Most people are totally unaware of what lightning is, how it behaves and what it can do," he said. "Take the old wives' tale about lightning never hitting the same place twice—a common enough belief. It's totally false. As a matter of fact, if a place has been hit once, it shows that it is a prime site for future strikes."

Pelletier also says that many people believe their homes to be safe from lightning because of the proximity of tall trees or a high television aerial. Neither is necessarily true.

We can thank Ben Franklin's inquisitive (and financially long-sighted) mind for the protection we now have against destruction of property caused by lightning.

"It has pleased God in His goodness to mankind, at length to discover to them the means of securing their habitations and other buildings from mischief by thunder and lightning," wrote Franklin in the 1753 edition of *Poor Richard's Almanack*. He went on to outline a system that not only worked, but which remains, almost unchanged, as the most efficient form of lightning protection.

The heart of a lightning protection system is a series of rods extending at least 12 inches above a structure at lightning vulnerable places: peaks, gable ends, chimneys, etc.

These lightning rods (or "air terminals" in the jargon of lightning experts) are connected to each other by a woven copper cable roughly one-half inch thick. The cable, in turn, is grounded on at least two sides of the building to rods driven 10 feet into the earth, although the depth will vary somewhat in accordance with soil conditions. It is often said that a lightning rod gives protection within a circle whose radius is the height of the tip of the rod from the ground. Unfortunately, lightning does not always adhere to this rule, but the Canadian Standards Association says that "a properly installed lightning rod system, if not 100 per cent effective, will ensure that in nearly all cases of lightning strikes to buildings, little or no damage will result."

Fire statistics support these claims: in 1975, the most recent year for which figures are available, only 91 of the 2,559 structural fires started by lightning in Ontario occurred in buildings protected by lightning rod systems.

Pelletier explains that a properly working lightning rod system creates an easy route for the electrical charges to follow, diverting them away from the building and allowing them to dissipate harmlessly in the ground.

This, of course, is preferable to the unprotected alternative—where the bolt strikes the roof of the building and passes through the structure itself, leaping through walls, appliances, plumbing fixtures, radiators (and in some cases human beings) en route to the earth....

Your chances of being killed by lightning this summer are roughly one in a million—certainly no reason to cancel plans for boating, picnics and hiking during the warm season, but reason enough to implement precautions.

An electrical storm that swept the New York City area took a typical toll of human victims. A golfer whose foursome had sought refuge from the rain beneath a tree (a common mistake that accounts for one-third of thunderstorm fatalities) died when lightning slammed into the tree. His companions were unharmed. The storm's next victim was a fisherman holding a metal casting rod. Lightning leapt from the rod to his jacket zipper. His single companion was injured but recovered. The final victim, a young man, died while standing near a beachhouse.

All of these deaths could have been prevented had the victims followed commonsense safety measures.

A car is perhaps the safest place to be during an electrical storm. There have been few, if any, substantiated cases of lightning striking an automobile, but laboratory experiments show that the charge would pass harmlessly over the metal shell of the car and then leap from the undercarriage to the pavement.

Second only to a car (and virtually 100 per cent safe) is a dry building protected by lightning rods. When the first signs of thunder make themselves manifest, the sensible thing to do is go straight to the shelter of a protected building. Two-thirds of lightning-caused deaths occur outdoors.

When you are caught by a storm in an open area, do not, under any circumstances, take shelter under an isolated tree. If you cannot reach a protected building, seek a low-lying area of open land.

Trees are favourite targets for lightning, and electrical charges that surge from the base of a struck tree can kill for a considerable distance.

In one instance, a single bolt of lightning struck a tree in a Utah pasture and killed 500 sheep. There are recorded cases of cattle being killed while standing 100 yards from a struck tree.

Few people are killed by direct lightning strikes. If someone were directly hit, he would be severely burned. In most cases, the lightning victim is not burned but dies because currents cast off from a nearby lightning strike pass through his body, stopping his breathing and heartbeat.

Lightning frequently strikes water and electrical charges travel freely through this medium. Boats are high on the list of undesirable places to be when there is an approaching electrical storm. If you are in a boat, get to shore immediately and move some distance inland; shoreline trees are prime candidates for lightning strikes.

Swimmers, too, are in danger of being injured or killed by electrical charges that surge through water as a result of lightning.

If you find yourself in a protected house at the outbreak of a thunderstorm, take heart; you are safe.

Still, it is wise to stay away from sinks and bathtubs—your plumbing system is connected to a metal vent pipe protruding through the roof and is a potential lightning target.

Avoid touching refrigerators, stoves and other large metal objects. Do not use telephones or other electrical appliances, and stay away from stovepipes, chimneys and fireplaces. Windows and doors should be closed.

If your home or one of your outbuildings is struck by lightning, an immediate check-over is due to insure that no hidden fires have started. (Old-timers often referred to hot and cold lightning—the former causing fires and the latter merely hitting with one explosive bolt.) When lightning fells a human, it is often possible to revive him with prolonged artificial respiration. Many victims have recovered fully, while others were left with sight or hearing impairments.

But even when nestled in the security of a snug, lightning-protected house, there are still some people who find themselves quivering under the bed with the dog at the faintest rumble of thunder. This unfortunate segment of the population might consider moving to the Arctic or Antarctic—areas which see only one thunderstorm per decade.

If relocation does not fit your plans, we can only offer the slim comfort of words spoken by one lightning protection expert: "If you heard the thunder, the lightning did not strike you. If you saw the lightning, it missed you; and if it did strike you, you would not have known it."

Thought

1. Complete your list of lightning facts with additional information presented by the author.
2. Describe the process which culminates in an electrical storm.
3. Explain the physics involved in a lightning discharge.
4. Make a list from the essay of common misconceptions about lightning. Account for the prevalence of these misconceptions.

Style and Structure

5. The essay presents an abundance of facts about lightning. Through what devices does the author attract and maintain a reader's interest in her analysis of lightning?

Response and Extension

6. Devise a method to harness the energy of lightning. Your method may or may not be based on scientific data. Write an analytical essay outlining the process.
7. Write a short story which centres on an experience with lightning.

Words and Experience

Ted Hughes

- What is a word?
- Recall a notable event from your life and list five words which you would use to describe it.
- Narrate the event to the members of your group.
- Show your group the words you have listed and ask them to suggest others.

Sitting in a chair is simple enough, and seems to need no commentary. To see an aircraft cross the sky, while a crow flies in the opposite direction, is simple enough, and again we do not feel compelled to remark on it. To read a letter from the other side of the world, and then go and collect the debt it asks us to collect from somebody near, may not be so easy, but it needs no commentary. We do not need to describe to ourselves every step, very carefully, before we are able to take it. Words need not come into it. We imagine the whole situation, and the possible ways of dealing with it, and then proceed in the way that seems best. Our imagination works in scenes, things, little stories and people's feelings. If we imagine what someone will say, in reply to something we intend to say or do, we have first to imagine how they will feel. We are as a rule pretty confident we know how they will feel. We may be terribly wrong, of course, but at least we never doubt that it is what they feel which counts. And we can think like this without ever forming a single word in our heads. Many people, perhaps most of us, do think in words all the time, and keep a perpetual running commentary going or a mental conversation, about everything that comes under our attention or about something in the back of our minds. But it is not essential. And the people who think in dumb pictures and dim sensings seem to manage just as well. Maybe they manage even better. You can imagine who is likely to be getting most out of reading the gospels, for instance: the one who discusses every sentence word by word and argues the contradictions and questions every obscurity and challenges every absurdity, or the one who imagines, if only for a few seconds, but with the shock of full reality, just what it must have been like to be standing near when the woman touched Christ's garment and he turned round.

It is the same with all our experience of life: the actual substance of it, the material facts of it, embed themselves in us quite a long way from the world of words. It is when we set out to find words for some seemingly quite simple experience that we begin to realize what a huge gap there is between our understanding of what happens around us and inside us, and the words we have at our command to say something about it.

Words are tools, learned late and laboriously and easily forgotten, with which we try to give some part of our experience a more or less permanent shape outside ourselves. They are unnatural, in a way, and far from being ideal for their job. For one thing, a word has its own definite meanings. A word is its own little solar system of meanings. Yet we are wanting it to carry some part of our meaning, of the meaning of our experience, and the meaning of our experience is finally unfathomable, it reaches into our toes and back to before we were born and into the atom, with vague shadows and changing features, and elements that no expression of any kind can take hold of. And this is true of even the simplest experiences.

For instance, with that crow flying across, beneath the aeroplane, which I instanced as a very simple sight—how are we going to give our account of that? Forgetting for a moment the aircraft, the sky, the world beneath, and our own concerns—how are we to say what we see in the crow's flight? It is not enough to say the crow flies purposefully, or heavily, or rowingly, or whatever. There are no words to capture the infinite depth of crowiness in the crow's flight. All we can do is use a word as an indicator, or a whole bunch of words as a general directive. But the ominous thing in the crow's flight, the barefaced, bandit thing, the tattered beggarly gipsy thing, the caressing and shaping yet slightly clumsy gesture of the downstroke, as if the wings were both too heavy and too powerful, and the headlong sort of merriment, the macabre pantomime ghoulishness and the undertaker sleekness—you could go on for a very long time with phrases of that sort and still have completely missed your instant, glimpse knowledge of the world of the crow's wingbeat. And a bookload of such descriptions is immediately rubbish when you look up and see the crow flying.

Nevertheless, there are more important things than crows to try and say something about. Yet that is an example of how words tend to shut out the simplest things we wish to say. In a way, words are continually trying to displace our experience. And in so far as they are stronger than the raw life of our experience, and full of themselves and all the dictionaries they have digested, they do displace it.

But that is enough for the moment about the wilfulness of words. What about our experience itself, the stuff we are trying to put into words—is that so easy to grasp? It may seem a strange thing to say, but do we ever know what we really do know?

A short time ago, a tramp came to our door and asked for money. I gave him something and watched him walk away. That would seem to be a simple enough experience, watching a tramp walk away. But how could I begin to describe what I saw? As with the crow, words seem suddenly a bit thin. It is not enough to say "The tramp walked away" or even "The tramp went away with a slinking sort of shuffle, as if he wished he were running full speed for the nearest corner". In ordinary descriptive writing such phrases have to suffice, simply because the writer has to economize on time, and if he set down everything that is to be seen in a man's walk he would never get on to the next thing, there would not be room, he would have written a whole biography, that would be the book. And even then, again just as with the crow, he would have missed the most important factor: that what he saw, he saw and understood in one flash, a single 1,000-volt shock, that lit up everything and drove it into his bones, whereas in such words and phrases he is dribbling it out over pages in tinglings that can only just be felt.

What *do* we see in a person's walk? I have implied that we see everything, the whole biography. I believe this is in some way true. How we manage it, nobody knows. Maybe some instinctive and involuntary mimicry within us reproduces that person at first glance, imitates him so exactly that we feel at once all he feels, all that gives that particular uniqueness to the way he walks or does what he is doing. Maybe there is more to it. But however it works, we get the information.

It is one thing to get the information, and quite another to become conscious of it, to know that we have got it. In our brains there are many mansions, and most of the doors are locked, with the keys inside. Usually, from our first meeting with a person, we get some single main impression, of like or dislike, confidence or distrust, reality or artificiality, or some single, vivid something that we cannot pin down in more than a tentative, vague phrase. That little phrase is like the visible moving fin of a great fish in a dark pool: we can see only the fin: we cannot see the fish, let alone catch or lift it out. Or usually we cannot. Sometimes we can. And some people have a regular gift for it.

I remember reading that the novelist H.E. Bates was in the habit of inventing quick brief biographies or adventures for people he met or saw who struck his imagination. Some of these little fantasies he noted down, to use in his stories. But as time passed, he discovered that these so-called fantasies were occasionally literal and accurate accounts of the lives of those very individuals he had seen. The odd thing about this, is that when he first invented them, he had thought it was all just imagination, that he was making it all up. In other words, he had received somehow or other accurate information, in great detail, by just looking—but hadn't recognized it for what it was. He had simply found it lying there in his mind, at that moment, unlabelled.

The great Swiss psycho-analyst Jung describes something similar in his autobiography. During a certain conversation, he wanted to illustrate some general point he was trying to make, and so just for an example he invented a fictitious character and set him in a fictitious situation and described his probable actions—all to illustrate his point. The man to whom he was speaking, somebody he had never met before, became terribly upset, and Jung could not understand why, until later, when he learned that the little story he had invented had been in fact a detailed circumstantial account of that man's own private life. Somehow or other, as they talked, Jung had picked it up—but without recognizing it. He had simply found it when he reached into his imagination for any odd materials that would make up a story of the kind he wanted.

Neither of these two men would have realized what they had learned if they had not both had occasion to invent stories on the spot, and if they had not by chance discovered later that what had seemed to them pure imagination had also somehow been fact. Neither had recognized their own experience. Neither had known what they really knew.

There are records of individuals who have the gift to recognize their experience at once, when it is of this sort. At first meeting with a stranger, such people sometimes see his whole life in a few seconds, like a film reeling past, in clear pictures. When this happens, they cannot help it. They simply see it, and know at once that it belongs to this person in front of them. Jung and Bates also saw it, but did not know—and they saw it only in an odd way, when they compelled themselves to produce a story at that very moment. And I believe we all share this sort of reception, this sort of experience, to some degree.

There are other individuals who have the gift to recognize in themselves not simply experience of this sort, but even a similar insight into the past lives and adventures of objects. Such people are known as psychometrists, and have been used by the police. From some weapon or tool used in a crime, they can as it were read off a description of the criminal and often a great deal about him. They are not infallible. But the best of them have amazing records of successes. They take hold of the particular object and the knowledge they are after flashes across their imaginations. Again, it is said by some that this is a gift we all share, potentially, that it is simply one of the characteristics of being alive in these mysterious electrical bodies of ours, and the difficult thing is not to pick up the information but to recognize it—to accept it into our consciousness. But this is not surprising. Most of us find it difficult to know what we are feeling about anything. In any situation, it is almost impossible to know what is really happening to us. This is one of the penalties of being human and having a brain so swarming with interesting suggestions and ideas and self-distrust.

And so with my tramp, I was aware of a strong impression all right, which disturbed me for a long time after he had gone. But what exactly had I learned? And how could I begin to delve into the tangled, rather painful mass of whatever it was that stirred in my mind as I watched him go away.

And watching a tramp go away, even if you have just been subliminally burdened with his entire biography, is a slight experience compared to the events that are developing in us all the time, as our private history and our personal make-up and hour by hour biological changes and our present immediate circumstances and all that we know, in fact, struggle together, trying to make sense of themselves in our single life, trying to work out exactly what is going on in and around us, and exactly what we are or could be, what we ought and ought not to do, and what exactly did happen in those situations which though we lived through them long since still go on inside us as if time could only make things fresher.

And all this is our experience. It is the final facts, as they are registered on this particular human measuring instrument. I have tried to suggest how infinitely beyond our ordinary notions of what we know our real knowledge, the real facts for us, really is. And to live removed from this inner universe of experience is also to live removed from ourself, banished from ourself and our real life. The struggle truly to possess his own experience, in other words to regain his genuine self, has been man's principal occupation, wherever he could find leisure for it, ever since he first grew this enormous surplus of brain. Men have invented religion to do this for others. But to do it for themselves, they have invented art—music, painting, dancing, sculpture, and the activity that includes all these, which is poetry.

Because it is occasionally possible, just for brief moments, to find the words that will unlock the doors of all those many mansions inside the head and express something—perhaps not much, just something—of the crush of information that presses in on us from the way a crow flies over and the way a man walks and the look of a street and from what we did one day a dozen years ago. Words that will express something of the deep complexity that makes us precisely the way we are, from the momentary effect of the barometer to the force that created men distinct from trees. Something of the inaudible music that moves us along in our bodies from moment to moment like water in a river. Something of the spirit of the snowflake in the water of the river. Something of the duplicity and the relativity and the merely fleeting quality of all this. Something of the almighty importance of it and something of the utter meaninglessness. And when words can manage something of this, and manage it in a moment of time, and in that same moment make out of it all the vital signature of a human being—not of an atom, or of a geometrical diagram, or of a heap of lenses—but a human being, we call it poetry.

Thought

1. Summarize and evaluate Hughes' view of the relationship between words and experience by examining specific sentences from his essay.

2. To what extent do you agree with the thought expressed in the following sentence: "And to live removed from this inner universe of experience is also to live removed from ourself, banished from ourself and our real life"?

3. According to Hughes, why have human beings invented the arts? Do you agree with him? Explain.

Style and Structure

4. Examine the anecdotes concerning the tramp, H.E. Bates, and Jung. Which of these anecdotes best serves his analysis of the process of translating experience into words?

5. Note the structure of the sentences comprising the final paragraph. How do these sentences anticipate the author's conclusion?

Response and Extension

6. In your journal, recount an incident from your personal experience which illustrates "how words tend to shut out the simplest things we wish to say."

7. Choose one word which has particular power or significance for you. Write an essay which analyses this word and its relationship to you.

Unit Synthesis

1. As a group, collect several poems which contain intense anger. Analyse the poems and compare the various ways in which the poets have articulated their anger.

2. In a group, read several stories by H.E. Bates, Ernest Hemingway, Alice Munro, W.P. Kinsella, Somerset Maugham, Alden Nowlan, and Morley Callaghan. Analyse how these authors have depicted entire personalities through the description of a gesture or a line of dialogue.

3. Research a process which interests you. Write an essay which analyzes the causal relationships within that process, e.g., a tennis serve, a hurricane, fibre optics, an automobile engine, photosynthesis, a bee sting, jealousy.

Writing to Persuade

To persuade is to encourage someone to alter an attitude or change a behaviour. In a persuasive essay, the author states an opinion in the form of a thesis which is unavoidably biased. To be persuasive, the essay must argue logically from that thesis. This is not to say that the appeal is only intellectual, for when the author becomes impassioned about the subject the argument becomes emotional and ultimately demands a response from the reader.

"Almost anybody can learn to think or believe or know," argues e.e. cummings, "but not a single human being can be taught to feel."

Carol Kleiman argues from her outrage over discriminatory language. "The expression 'broken home' suggests that my children never had a chance in life because their father was not present, and what I did doesn't count. I *know* that's not true."

Lindsy Van Gelder, however, uses humour in her argument against gender-exclusive language in her essay, "The Great Person-Hole-Cover Debate."

In constructing her argument justifying woman's right to know, Mary Meigs refers to familiar archetypes: "I think of Pandora not as irresponsible and foolish but as a radical feminist, sister of Eve and Bluebeard's wives."

Bertrand Russell uses the apparent antithesis between individual liberty and public control to persuade his audience. "Those whose minds are dominated by fear of a relapse toward barbarism will emphasize the importance of law and order, while those who are inspired by the hope of an advance toward civilization will usually be more conscious of the need of individual initiative."

In arguing for a more progressive and humanistic educational system, Irving Layton claims that "little minds, dry, scholastic, pedantical, are not going to make the world over, or provide it with the intellectual light it requires to lead it out safely from our present-day moral and political dilemmas."

These six essays develop strong arguments, both rational and passionate, which address certain attitudes and values. The success of each essay depends on whether or not the reader is convinced, and thereby comes to share the author's opinion.

A Poet's Advice to Students

e.e. cummings

- Distinguish among thinking, believing and feeling.

A poet is somebody who feels, and who expresses his feeling through words.

This may sound easy. It isn't.

A lot of people think or believe or know they feel—but that's thinking or believing or knowing; not feeling. And poetry is feeling—not knowing or believing or thinking.

Almost anybody can learn to think or believe or know, but not a single human being can be taught to feel. Why? Because whenever you think or you believe or you know, you're a lot of other people; but the moment you feel, you're nobody-but-yourself.

To be nobody-but-yourself—in a world which is doing its best, night and day, to make you everybody else—means to fight the hardest battle which any human being can fight; and never stop fighting.

As for expressing nobody-but-yourself in words, that means working just a little harder than anybody who isn't a poet can possibly imagine. Why? Because nothing is quite as easy as using words like somebody else. We all of us do exactly this nearly all the time—and whenever we do it, we're not poets.

If, at the end of your first ten or fifteen years of fighting and working and feeling, you find you've written one line of one poem; you'll be very lucky indeed.

And so my advice to all young people who wish to become poets is: do something easy, like learning how to blow up the world—unless you're not only willing, but glad, to feel and work and fight till you die.

Does this sound dismal? It isn't.
It's the most wonderful life on earth.
Or so I feel.

Thought

1. Identify the three classes of people perceived by the writer. To which class do you belong? Explain.
2. Paraphrase cummings' definition of a poet.
3. What advice does cummings give to all young people? Do you agree or disagree with this advice?

Style and Structure

4. By examining his diction, determine whether the author is appealing primarily to the intellect or to the senses in attempting to persuade the reader of his point of view.
5. Label the parts of the argument using the following terms: thesis, support, development, commentary, clarification, conclusion.

Response and Extension

6. a) In your own words, define "nobody-but-yourself."
   b) Using cummings' essay as your model, write a persuasive essay about the importance of being "nobody-but-yourself."
7. In your journal, explain the major difficulties you have writing creatively.

The Great Person-Hole-Cover Debate

Lindsy Van Gelder

- Identify and discuss the ways in which the English language is "male-dominated."

I wasn't looking for trouble. What I was looking for, actually, was a little tourist information to help me plan a camping trip to New England.

But there it was, on the first page of the 1979 edition of the State of Vermont *Digest of Fish and Game Laws and Regulations*: a special message of welcome from one Edward F. Kehoe, commissioner of the Vermont Fish and Game Department, to the reader and would-be camper, *i.e.,* me.

This person (*i.e.,* me) is called "the sportsman."

"We have no 'sportswomen, sportspersons, sportsboys, or sportsgirls,'" Commissioner Kehoe hastened to explain, obviously anticipating that some of us sportsfeminists might feel a bit overlooked. "But," he added, "we are pleased to report that we do have many great sportsmen who are women, as well as young people of both sexes."

It's just that the Fish and Game Department is trying to keep things "simple and forthright" and to respect "long-standing tradition." And anyway, we really ought to be flattered, "sportsman" being "a meaningful title being earned by a special kind of dedicated man, woman, or young person, as opposed to just any hunter, fisherman, or trapper."

I have heard this particular line of reasoning before. In fact, I've heard it so often that I've come to think of it as The Great Person-Hole-Cover Debate, since gender-neutral manholes are invariably brought into the argument as evidence of the lengths to which humorless,

Newspeak-spouting feminists will go to destroy their mother tongue.

Consternation about womanhandling the language comes from all sides. Sexual conservatives who see the feminist movement as a unisex plot and who long for the good olde days of *vive la différence*, when men were men and women were women, nonetheless do not rally behind the notion that the term "mankind" excludes women.

But most of the people who choke on expressions like "spokesperson" aren't right-wing misogynists, and this is what troubles me. Like the undoubtedly well-meaning folks at the Vermont Fish and Game Department, they tend to reassure you right up front that they're only trying to keep things "simple" and to follow "tradition," and that some of their best men are women, anyway.

Usually they wind up warning you, with great sincerity, that you're jeopardizing the worthy cause of women's rights by focusing on "trivial" side issues. I would like to know how anything that gets people so defensive and resistant can possibly be called "trivial," whatever else it might be.

The English language is alive and constantly changing. Progress— both scientific and social—is reflected in our language, or should be.

Not too long ago, there was a product called "flesh-colored" Band-Aids. The flesh in question was colored Caucasian. Once the civil rights movement pointed out the racism inherent in the name, it was dropped. I cannot imagine reading a thoughtful, well-intentioned company policy statement explaining that while the Band-Aids would continue to be called "flesh-colored" for old time's sake, black and brown people would now be considered honorary whites and were perfectly welcome to use them.

Most sensitive people manage to describe our national religious traditions as "Judeo-Christian," even though it takes a few seconds longer to say than "Christian." So why is it such a hardship to say "he or she" instead of "he"?

I have a modest proposal for anyone who maintains that "he" is just plain easier: since "he" has been the style for several centuries now— and since it really includes everybody anyway, right?—it seems only fair to give "she" a turn. Instead of having to ponder over the intricacies of, say, "Congressman" versus "Congressperson" versus "Representative," we can simplify things by calling them all "Congresswoman."

Other clarifications will follow: "a woman's home is her castle"..."a giant step for all womankind"..."All women are created equal"... "Fisherwoman's Wharf."...

And don't be upset by the business letter that begins "Dear Madam," fellas. It means you, too.

Thought

1. Is Commissioner Kehoe's justification of his use of the word "sportsman" reasonable? Explain.
2. Why do people resist changing the language along the lines suggested by Van Gelder?
3. Why does the writer use issues relating to civil rights and religious traditions to illustrate her argument about language?

Style and Structure

4. Comment upon the appropriateness of the first sentence of "The Great Person-Hole-Cover Debate" as an introduction to a persuasive essay.
5. Select three examples of Van Gelder's humour. What do you conclude about Van Gelder's humour from these examples?

Response and Extension

6. Find examples of sexist language in recent publications. Report your findings to the class in an informal speech.
7. Is there ever justification for the continued use of gender-exclusive language? Write a persuasive essay arguing for or against its continued use.

Pandora Was a Feminist

Mary Meigs

- In groups, discuss why there are secrets. What makes a secret a secret?
- Do you find it hard to keep a secret? Why or why not?

Secrets. The origin of secrets—a great puzzle that I'm trying to solve, for it seems to me that there is an urgent need to decide which, if any, are necessary and which spring from the ego's need to protect its truths and its lies, hence, the idea that every self is a sacred place and that all secrets have the same sacred character. Other people's secrets, as we know, beg to be told, make up the fabric of gossip and innuendo even if severe penalties are attached to telling them. As for our own, they are raided, so to speak, by others with their conjectures, their analyses that we so fiercely reject (like ours of them). One's secret self is guarded as closely as spies guard secrets in wartime, not because of a real penalty for telling (unlike the spies), but an imaginary one, because of the feeling that it belongs to oneself, like one's brain, one's heart, and the illusion that it is invisible to others. But, in fact, those others are nibbling away, like fishes around bait, so that it might be better to give them an authentic whole to nibble on. Better still, perhaps, to sit in one of those cages in which one is completely visible but protected from over-eager sharks, the cage of indifference to what other people think. I often wonder if the secret of oneself is worth keeping, if it shouldn't be released like the contents of Pandora's box. That story is a wonderful example of patriarchal ingenuity, which has invented yet another mythical explanation for the woes of *man*kind, i.e. the unbridled curiosity of womankind. Personally, I think of Pandora not as irresponsible and foolish but as a radical feminist, sister of Eve and Bluebeard's wives, of all women who *want to know*. We are all Pandoras, each with her box complete with instructions not to open it, the box of the secret self.

Pandora, according to Zimmerman's *Dictionary of Classical Mythology*, was made with clay by Hephaestus at the request of Zeus, who desired to punish Prometheus for stealing fire from heaven by giving him a wife. "All the gods and goddesses of Olympus vied in giving her gifts:" beauty, eloquence, the art of singing, beautiful clothes, a gold crown, etc., not to mention the famous box, a gift from Zeus himself. But Prometheus saw through Zeus, and Pandora ended by marrying his brother Epimetheus (which means Afterthought). "Don't open the box," said Zeus. Naturally, Pandora opened it. So do I open things: Christmas presents before Christmas, the last page of a book to see how it's going to end (I have to know whether it will have a happy ending, or whether so-and-so will still be alive at the end. I hate suspense, cannot read detective stories, cannot look at movies full of suspense without intolerable anxiety.) But to get back to Pandora. "When the box was opened, a host of plagues escaped to harass hapless man; only Hope remained in the box." Why? It seems to me it would have been much better to let Hope out, too. "Women's curiosity is always punished," I remarked to Paul, a male friend. "Pandora's, Eve's, Bluebeard's wives." "Of course," he says. "Evil is woman's fault. That's part of history." He's making fun of me, of course. I say I think people should be less possessive of their secrets, that Pandora was right to open the box. And then he tells me a fascinating story about himself. He used to dream, he says, to remember his dreams and write them down, until one day a dream told him something about himself that he didn't want to know. So he pushed it back into his subconscious. "And I never remembered another dream!" Pandora couldn't possibly have been more curious about the contents of her box than I am about this dream-truth that he doesn't want to think about. I say to him that nothing in my dreams makes me want to censure them, that there is nothing they tell me that I don't want to think about, that they have helped me to think about the things I don't want to think about. And far from wanting to turn them off, I want to stimulate them, I want them to tell me the worst!

Curiosity, how it can be thought of as either a virtue or a vice, how it is a virtue for men in men's eyes and a vice for women which must be punished, and how the punishment becomes dogma until women, too, feel impatient with Eve, Pandora and Bluebeard's wives for being so foolish, for wanting to know. God or Zeus or Bluebeard loves to tempt them by inventing rules that as high-spirited women, they are bound to break. Don't eat of the fruit of the tree! Don't open that box! Don't look in the closet! Sometimes God, just for good measure, tests a man. Don't ask me *why*, he says to Job. But much more often, men's curiosity is rewarded and women's is punished. And yet when it comes to opening the Pandora's box which is in each of us, men and women are alike.

Paul's self-censorship—the Pandora's box of his dreams—he seemed to think it was wrong to know *too much* about himself and called on the Zeus in himself to close the box forever. I wondered how often he had told this story, whether each telling wasn't to reinforce the lock, whether the *thing* he wanted to shut away didn't manage to reach out a paw under the lid like an angry kitten in a basket. He told it smiling, with a kind of excitement, triumph, ha! *it* almost got out! It seemed to me that *it* was amazingly discreet; it could be talked about without betraying what it was even to Paul. Perhaps it had become so tame that it was ready to be let out of the box; perhaps he told it as a way of taming it?

I think about *it*, the beast, silenced but still there in the dreams that are not allowed over the threshold of consciousness, and want to say, "Let it out. It won't hurt you," want to say that secrets, once released, often sheath their claws, stretch, rub against other people's ankles and finally curl up in a comfortable chair and go to sleep. Interestingly, Pandora was not punished (note that the plagues "escaped to harass hapless *man*"). Long after the affair of the box, Zeus sent a deluge to destroy *man*kind and Pandora's daughter, Pyrrha, and her husband, Deucalion (Prometheus' son), were the only survivors. They had the foresight to replace "the loss of mankind by throwing stones behind their backs; those Deucalion threw became men; those Pyrrha threw became women." So the sexes, each reproduced by a kind of parthenogenesis (another case of patriarchal wish-fulfillment), were equal for a while, and Pandora was the grandmother of all the women in the world. True, the "host of plagues" was still at large, but Zeus himself had invented them and put them in the box, a cover-up, so to speak, and Pandora had the courage to show everybody what Zeus was up to. It was a tremendous victory over Zeus, just as Eve had won a victory over God by disobeying his senseless edict about eating the fruit of the tree. Confronted by boxes that are not supposed to be opened, we contemporary Pandoras say to ourselves, "Where did this rule come from? Was it Zeus who told me not open the box, and is he impersonating me so skillfully that I think his commands come from myself?"

Thought

1. Paraphrase and explain the "great puzzle" that Meigs is trying to solve.
2. What does the author mean by "the secret of oneself"?
3. Analyze the relationship between the "secret of oneself" and "Pandora's Box" for a) Paul, b) the author.

4. Why, in the author's view, was Pandora a feminist? Do you agree?
5. In what sense did Pandora score a victory over Zeus?

Style and Structure

6. How does the author attempt to persuade the reader that there is a definite relationship among Eve, Pandora, and Bluebeard's wives?
7. Stylistically, how does the author involve herself in this relationship?
8. Examine the stylistic use the author makes of her references to her friend Paul.
9. What effects are achieved by the concluding sentence of the essay?

Response and Extension

10. Write a critical essay which examines a fairy tale from a feminist perspective, e.g., "Cinderella," "Sleeping Beauty," "Rapunzel," "Beauty and the Beast."
11. Debate the following statement: "Little Red Riding Hood" is nothing but a children's fairy tale.

My Home Is Not Broken, It Works

Carol Kleiman

- Discuss the connotations of the expression "broken home."
- Identify ways our society discriminates against single-parent families.

One summer day, my son Robert, then five years old, took me by the hand and asked me to go outside with him.

Holding on tightly, he carefully walked around the house with me, looking at doors and windows and shaking his head. There was something he didn't understand.

"Mommy," he finally asked, pressing my hand with his warm, chubby fingers, "is our home broken?"

His words shot through my body, alerting every protective instinct, activating my private defense system, the one I hold in reserve to ward off attacks against women and children.

"Oh, Robbie," I answered, hugging him, "did someone tell you that we have a broken home?"

"Yes," he said sweetly. "But it doesn't *look* broken!"

"It's not," I assured him. "Our house is not broken and neither are we."

I explained that "broken" is some people's way of describing a home with only one parent, usually the mother. Sometimes there was only one parent because of divorce, like us. "There are still lots of homes like ours. And they're still homes."

Robbie looked relieved and went to play with his friends. I stood there, shaking with anger.

What a way to put down a little kid and me, too, I thought. I supported my three children, fed and clothed them. I was there for them emotionally and physically. I managed to keep up payments on the house. Although we struggled financially, we were happy and loving. What was "broken" about us?

That was in 1970. The expression is as prevalent today as it was then. We've made some headway in raising the issue of sexist expressions, including such formerly popular ones as calling women "girls," "gals," or "broads." We've even sensitized a few headline writers to their unhealthy habit of describing women as "grandmothers" and "mothers" while the stories about them are totally unrelated to their biological roles. Such as: "Grandmother Elected Prime Minister."

But a household headed by a woman is still a "broken home," despite the fact that more than 5 million women raise their families alone. A residence in which a man is not in residence, the phrase implies, is not a home. Two decades into the second wave of the Women's Movement, the phrase is often used as an explanation for a terrible crime, as if a woman alone were disreputable and can only raise a vicious miscreant who will naturally prey upon society: "The alleged murderer is a loner and comes from a broken home."

Over the years, similar buzzwords have sent me buzzing. Even though I work for a newspaper and understand how journalists are misunderstood, I am constantly writing letters of protest to publications that deprecate me and all women with frequent use of expressions such as "divorcée," "unwed" mother, and "illegitimate" children. They have something offensively in common: they tell us that if no husband/ father exists, neither do women and children.

It's true that society does not help single or divorced women raise their children or keep their families intact. The scorn felt for so-called broken homes is expressed in the lack of support systems for heads of those households, in the withholding of federally funded quality child care, job training and equal pay, and in the meanness with which aid to dependent children is doled out.

The expression "broken home" suggests that my children never had a chance in life because their father was not present, and what I did doesn't count. I *know* that's not true, and it's not true for millions of other Americans also stigmatized by the term.

I had some testimony recently that I am not alone in my strong belief that my house is truly a home. It came from my three children.

On a recent Thanksgiving, my trio—Catharine, then 21; Raymond, Jr., 19; and Robert, 18—gathered in Chicago for the holiday. After they left, I found a note on my desk that they had written and signed before dispersing to their various colleges from coast to coast.

It begins: "Yet another Thanksgiving holiday has drawn our family together for a few meaningful days. It's just enough time to touch base, strengthen our bond, and reaffirm how important we are to one another.''

As I read on, I remembered Robbie's question a dozen years ago and how much it hurt. Here was the real answer to the question: Is our home broken? The note ended: "We thank you for making us what we are."

Thought

1. Why was Kleiman so angry over the incident involving her son?
2. List the expressions which Kleiman finds sexist and/or demeaning. Explain the connotations associated with each expression. Suggest alternatives for these expressions.
3. List and discuss other expressions which you find to be sexist and/or demeaning.

Style and Structure

4. How do Kleiman's anecdotes about her children add to the persuasive nature of the essay?
5. How does Kleiman make this essay more than just a vent for her anger?

Response and Extension

6. Prepare a report on the legal process involved in the dissolution of marriage. Your report should take into consideration the latest developments in family law, both in federal and provincial legislation.

Individual Liberty and Public Control

Bertrand Russell

- What are the individual's responsibilities to society?
- What are society's responsibilities to the individual?

Society cannot exist without law and order, and cannot advance except through the initiative of vigorous innovators. Yet law and order are always hostile to innovations, and innovators are almost always to some extent anarchists. Those whose minds are dominated by fear of a relapse toward barbarism will emphasize the importance of law and order, while those who are inspired by the hope of an advance toward civilization will usually be more conscious of the need of individual initiative. Both temperaments are necessary, and wisdom lies in allowing each to operate freely where it is beneficent. But those who are on the side of law and order, since they are reinforced by custom and the instinct for upholding the *status quo*, have no need of a reasoned defense. It is the innovators who have difficulty in being allowed to exist and work. Each generation believes that this difficulty is a thing of the past, but each generation is tolerant only of *past* innovations. Those of its own day are met with the same persecution as if the principle of toleration had never been heard of.

On any matter of general interest, there is usually in any given community, at any given time, a received opinion, which is accepted as a matter of course by all who give no special thought to the matter. Any questioning of the received opinion arouses hostility, for a number of reasons.

The most important of these is the instinct of conventionality, which exists in all gregarious animals, and often leads them to put to death any markedly peculiar member of the herd. The next most important is the feeling of insecurity aroused by doubt as to the beliefs by which we are in the habit of regulating our lives. Whoever has tried to explain the philosophy of Berkeley to a plain man will have seen in its unadulterated form the anger aroused by this feeling. What the plain man derives from Berkeley's philosophy at a first hearing is an uncomfortable suspicion that nothing is solid, so that it is rash to sit on a chair or to expect the floor to sustain us. Because this suspicion is uncomfortable it is irritating, except to those who regard the whole argument as merely nonsense. And in a more or less analogous way any questioning of what has been taken for granted destroys the feeling of standing on solid ground, and produces a condition of bewildered fear.

A third reason which makes men dislike novel opinions is, that vested interests are bound up with old beliefs. The long fight of the Church against science, from Giordano Bruno to Darwin, is attributable to this motive, among others. The horror of socialism which existed in the remote past was entirely attributable to this case. But it would be a mistake to assume, as is done by those who seek economic motives everywhere, that vested interests are the principal source of anger against novelties in thought. If this were the case, intellectual progress would be much more rapid than it is. The instinct of conventionality, horror of uncertainty, and vested interests, all militate against the acceptance of a new idea. And it is even harder to think of a new idea than to get it accepted: most people might spend a lifetime in reflection without ever making a genuinely original discovery.

In view of all these obstacles, it is not likely that any society at any time will suffer from a plethora of heretical opinions. Least of all is this likely in a modern civilized society, where the conditions of life are in constant rapid change, and demand, for successful adaptation, an equally rapid change in intellectual outlook. There should, therefore, be an attempt to encourage rather than discourage the expression of new beliefs and the dissemination of knowledge tending to support them. But the very opposite is in fact the case. From childhood upwards, everything is done to make the minds of men and women conventional and sterile. And if, by misadventure, some spark of imagination remains, its unfortunate possessor is considered unsound and dangerous, worthy only of contempt in time of peace and of prison or a traitor's death in time of war. Yet such men are known to have been in the past the chief benefactors of mankind, and are the very men who receive most honor as soon as they are safely dead.

The whole realm of thought and opinion is utterly unsuited to public control: it ought to be as free, and as spontaneous, as is possible to those who know what others have believed. The state is justified in insisting that children shall be educated, but it is not justified in forcing their education to proceed on a uniform plan and to be directed to the production of a dead level of glib uniformity. Education, and the life of the mind generally, is a matter in which individual initiative is the chief thing needed; the function of the state should begin and end with insistence on *some* kind of education, and, if possible, a kind which promotes mental individualism, not a kind which happens to conform to the prejudices of government officials.

II

Questions of practical morals raise more difficult problems than questions of mere opinion. The Thugs of India honestly believe it their duty to commit murders, but the government does not acquiesce. Conscientious objectors honestly hold the opposite opinion, and again the government does not acquiesce. The punishment of conscientious objectors seems clearly a violation of individual liberty within its legitimate sphere.

It is generally assumed without question that the state has a right to punish certain kinds of sexual irregularity. No one doubts that the Mormons sincerely believed polygamy to be a desirable practice, yet the United States required them to abandon its legal recognition, and probably any other Christian country would have done likewise. Nevertheless, I do not think this prohibition was wise. Polygamy is legally permitted in many parts of the world, but is not much practiced except by chiefs and potentates. I think that in all such cases the law should intervene only when there is some injury inflicted without the consent of the injured person.

It is obvious that men and women would not tolerate having their wives or husbands selected by the state, whatever eugenists might have to say in favor of such a plan. In this, it seems clear that ordinary public opinion is in the right, not because people choose wisely, but because any choice of their own is better than a forced marriage. What applies to marriage ought also to apply to the choice of a trade or profession: although some men have no marked preferences, most men greatly prefer some occupations to others, and are far more likely to be useful citizens if they follow their preferences than if they are thwarted by a public authority.

III

We may now arrive at certain general principles in regard to individual liberty and public control.

The greater part of human impulses may be divided into two classes, those which are possessive and those which are constructive or creative.

Property is the direct expression of possessiveness; science and art are among the most direct expressions of creativeness. Possessiveness is either defensive or aggressive; it seeks either to retain something against a robber, or to acquire something from a present holder. In either case, an attitude of hostility to others is of its essence.

The whole realm of the possessive impulses, and of the use of force to which they give rise, stands in need of control by a public neutral authority, in the interests of liberty no less than of justice. Within a nation, this public authority will naturally be the state; in relations between nations, if the present anarchy is to cease, it will have to be some international parliament. But the motive underlying the public control of men's possessive impulses should always be the increase of liberty, both by the prevention of private tyranny, and by the liberation of creative impulses. If public control is not to do more harm than good, it must be so exercised as to leave the utmost freedom of private initiative in all ways that do not involve the private use of force. In this respect, all governments have always failed egregiously, and there is no evidence that they are improving.

The creative impulses, unlike those that are possessive, are directed to ends in which one man's gain is not another man's loss. The man who makes a scientific discovery or writes a poem is enriching others at the same time as himself. Any increase in knowledge or good-will is a gain to all who are affected by it, not only to the actual possessor. Force cannot create such things, though it can destroy them; no principle of distributive justice applies to them, since the gain of each is the gain of all. For these reasons, the creative part of a man's activity ought to be as free as possible from all public control, in order that it may remain spontaneous and full of vigor. The only function of the state in regard to this part of the individual life should be to do everything possible toward providing outlets and opportunities.

Huge organizations, both political and economic, are one of the distinguishing characteristics of the modern world. These organizations have immense power, and often use their power to discourage originality in thought and action. They ought, on the contrary, to give the freest scope that is possible without producing anarchy or violent conflict.

The problem which faces the modern world is the combination of individual initiative with the increase in the scope and size of organizations. Unless it is solved, individuals will grow less and less full of life and vigor, more and more passively submissive to conditions imposed upon them. A society composed of such individuals cannot be progressive, or add much to the world's stock of mental and spiritual possessions.

Only personal liberty and the encouragement of initiative can secure these things. Those who resist authority when it encroaches upon the legitimate sphere of the individual are performing a service to society, however little society may value it. In regard to the past, this is universally acknowledged; but it is no less true in regard to the present and the future.

Thought

1. Explain the paradox contained in the first two sentences of the essay.

2. According to Russell, why are innovators at a disadvantage?

3. How does Russell account for the hostility which greets someone who questions received opinion? Discuss a contemporary figure whose reception supports Russell's argument.

4. Do you agree with Russell's contention that "the function of the state should begin and end with insistence on *some* kind of education, and, if possible, a kind which promotes mental individualism"?

5. Outline the differences, in Russell's view, between possessiveness and creativity. Are these differences valid?

6. Do you agree that "those who resist authority when it encroaches upon the legitimate sphere of the individual are performing a service to society"? Explain.

Style and Structure

7. Russell cites no statistics, states few facts, and appeals to no authority other than himself. How, then, does he make his essay so persuasive?

8. Russell divides his essay into three sections. Summarize the organizing idea for each section.

Response and Extension

9. Debate the following statement: "From childhood upwards, everything is done to make the minds of men and women conventional and sterile."

10. Write a personal essay which examines the limits of your own choices.

The Role of the Teacher

Irving Layton

- What do you want your education to do for you?
- What is the etymology of the word "education"? Discuss.
- List and discuss the traits exhibited by the excellent teacher.

In the past few years, educational institutions have been under severe attack. As the volume of criticism has mounted, a feeling has grown that schools and universities are not achieving that which they were intended to: namely, the enrichment of the individual's life by giving him the tools of self-improvement and the cultivated mind to use them. Naturally the bulk of this criticism has fallen upon the teacher, that poor cultural maid-of-all-work in our society, and the nearest, or at any rate, the most tangible object to seize upon in a fit of anger. Of course the fault does not lie there, or not mainly. Often it lies with unprogressive or penny-pinching school boards who engage teachers whose unsuitability is fully known to them in advance. And behind the incompetent teacher and the conservative school board stands a society which has no comprehensive vision of what education is or the aims that it ought to pursue. If we're going to start blaming, let's call the shots right.

No instructed observer denies that there are proportionately fewer general readers today than even twenty-five years ago. To increasingly larger numbers, books have become objects of curiosity; like an atomic pile, something heard about but hardly ever seen. In such a situation, the hardest hit have been the humanities. While every kind of narrow specialism is having a field day, the generous disciplines of the mind, philosophy, art, literature, are being discarded like old running-shoes. A constricted scientism, lacking both a sense of direction and a concern for values, has penetrated every nook and cranny of our society. The end of this process no one yet foresees, but already institutions of liberal learning are fast becoming anachronistic.

Little minds, dry, scholastic, pedantical, are not going to make the world over, or provide it with the intellectual light it requires to lead it out safely from our present-day moral and political dilemmas. Nor little hearts, untouched by concern for humanity. If education means anything, it should mean the creation of individuals with a strong sense of social responsibility, a regard for people, an attitude of helpfulness towards them that springs from an imaginative awareness of human need. In the long run, it means education for individual and collective freedom. A society where such persons abounded would place its mystics, seers, and artists in the front rank for they do the two things most vitally needed by an "open society": they interpret and help to shape the moral conscience of the human race, and they continuously enlarge the boundaries of human sensibility.

These reflections lead one to assay the role of the teacher. Without beating about the bush, let it be said at the outset that his function is paramount. Nowadays it's the usual thing to pay lip service in praise of the teacher's significance and utility—particularly on graduation day or when the cornerstone for a new school building is being laid; for the rest of the year he is grossly undervalued, underpaid, and almost all but forgotten. Yet his, nevertheless, is the power and the glory. His influence is incalculable, extending beyond the one or two years during which a teacher may have a particular class. It is usually from a gifted teacher that a child catches his first glimpse of harmony or wisdom and gets his first hint of the intellectual adventure which may engage him for the rest of his life.

But for a teacher to communicate the vision of the good life, he must first have that vision himself. If his own light does not burn steadily, he can not hope to kindle it in any one else. A teacher—what is he, if not an inspired seeker after the truth? In teaching as in the writing of poetry, techniques and formulae may support, but can never supplant inspiration.

Only by pursuing knowledge, that is, by constantly enlarging his own intellectual horizons, can the teacher retain his original freshness and enthusiasm. In the successfully creative teacher, knowledge spills over like water from a seemingly inexhaustible fountain. This kind of teacher is always an inspiration to his pupils. Furthermore the knowledge which he acquires in his free time and which he shares with others eventually trickles into the remotest corners of the community he lives in and helps to enlarge the area of good sense upon which the preservation of civilized values ultimately depends.

Thought

1. According to Layton, for what reasons are educational institutions "under severe attack"?
2. According to Layton, who deserves to be blamed for the perceived shortcomings of educational institutions?
3. Do you agree that "the generous disciplines of the mind, philosophy, art, literature, are being discarded"? Explain.
4. Do you agree that the sciences are "lacking both a sense of direction and a concern for values"?
5. a) Paraphrase Layton's definition of education contained within the third paragraph.
   b) Would this kind of education produce the society Layton envisions? Explain.
6. Do you agree with Layton's statement, "It is usually from a gifted teacher that a child catches his first glimpse of harmony or wisdom and gets his first hint of the intellectual adventure which may engage him for the rest of his life"? Discuss.

Style and Structure

7. a) Examine the diction Layton uses to describe those persons he views to be impediments to education.
   b) In your view, is such diction justified?
8. How do the first three paragraphs relate to the rest of the essay?

Response and Extension

9. Ask your school principal to read this essay. Invite your principal to your class to respond to the essay and present other philosophies of education.
10. Write an essay in which you respond to one of the statements made by your school principal.

Unit Synthesis

1. "The state is justified in insisting that children shall be educated, but it is not justified in forcing their education to proceed on a uniform plan and to be directed to the production of a dead level of glib uniformity." Write an essay which examines the degree to which the essays by cummings and Layton support Russell's opinion.

2. "There should...," says Russell, "be an attempt to encourage rather than discourage the expression of new beliefs and the dissemination of knowledge tending to support them." Write an essay which relates this statement to the ideas expressed by Van Gelder, Meigs, and Kleiman.

3. Research a prominent figure in the women's movement. Write an essay which presents information on her background, accomplishments, and ideas, and includes your evaluation of her ideas.

4. Write a persuasive essay which takes a stand on an important public issue, e.g., freedom of expression and access versus censorship; free enterprise versus state regulation of the marketplace; the public's right to know versus the individual's right to privacy.

WRITING TO REFLECT

"To think for yourself–not narrowly, but rather as a mind–you must be able to talk to yourself: well, honestly, and at length."

This statement by William H. Gass exemplifies many of the characteristics of the reflective essay: it is personal, contemplative, judgemental and self-justifying.

Frequently, the reflective essay is anecdotal. Often its anecdotes are confessional and leave the author vulnerable, seeking a resolution with some aspect of the past. This is seen for example in Anne Rivers Siddons' essay: "It was what we all were in the mid-fifties, we Revloned and duck-or-ponytailed young girls; were, or aspired to be. Cute."

Implicit in reflection is self-analysis. "I am a quiet, occasionally grim, somewhat ascetic man," writes Anthony Brandt of himself, "willing, I've always thought, to leave happiness to those lucky people who are born cheerful." For the essayist, such self-analysis is articulated in the hope that it will be of benefit to the essay's readers.

Phyllis Theroux, in reflecting upon her own attitudes and behaviour, comes to an understanding of her relationship with her daughter. "I decided that what my daughter wanted was immaterial. I wanted her to take piano lessons.... My daughter thinks I am cruel, that I don't understand her, that I am trying to force her to be something she is not. My daughter is right."

Northrop Frye reflects upon the way his relationship with society has changed over his lifetime: "The world I was born into in 1912 was both a stable world and a simple one, a world of ordered values, whereas now these values are being questioned or denied, and are either disappearing or turning into something else."

The purposes of reflection are as various as the authors who engage in it. All respond to Gass' exhortation, "How desperately we need to learn to talk to ourselves."

In Selfish Pursuit

Anthony Brandt

- What relationship exists for you among wealth, success, and happiness?

I want to talk about the pursuit of happiness and the dilemmas it leads us into. But I should explain my own bias, my old habit of contempt for this pursuit, before I begin. Until I looked up the history of the phrase not too long ago, I believed that happiness was an unworthy goal and couldn't understand why Jefferson gave it such weight when he wrote the Declaration of Independence. Life and liberty were inalienable rights clearly enough, but why the pursuit of happiness? Why not something more substantial, like greatness or knowledge?

As it turns out, Jefferson did not mean by happiness what we mean by it; we tend to think of happiness as a feeling, an entirely subjective delight, the inner grin that appears when life seems free of problems and disappears when they return. The pursuit of happiness so defined inevitably becomes a matter of managing one's internal state, one's moods. And my moods are characteristically, even genetically, somewhat dour. My father was a Swede by descent and as phlegmatic as that race is supposed to be. My mother was a fierce woman who more often inspired fear in me than delight. One day, I remember, I pulled a muscle so badly she had to take me to the doctor. Walking to the car, I started to groan from the pain; "Keep it to yourself," she snapped. I've hardly allowed myself to groan since. She was a stoic, and her stoicism became the model for my own. Over the years I developed a certain indifference to how I feel. I've lived with minor ailments for years and done nothing about them. I've come to believe that I should ignore my internal emotional state as well.

My whole disposition, in short, led me to this contempt for the pursuit of happiness. I am a quiet, occasionally grim, somewhat ascetic man, willing, I've always thought, to leave happiness to those lucky people who are born cheerful. I am of the type that has trouble letting go and having fun. I can't remember jokes when I've heard them. And life has always seemed to me a testing ground; like a fox crossing the ice or a soldier in a minefield, you proceed with great caution, take nothing for granted, and count yourself blessed just to have made it to the other side.

But I am a living contradiction; I am in fact—beneath the moods, the stoicism, the seriousness—a happy man. How so? It comes from the conditions of my life. My two children have grown up healthy, bright, and decent; I live in one of the loveliest villages in America. My wife loves and delights me, and I her. Most important of all, I believe to the center of my being that the work I am doing is the work I was meant to do. So this dour man, who can't dance, who worries that he drinks too much, is secretly pleased with himself and is free not to believe in the pursuit of happiness because he has already caught up with it.

I don't, however, feel entirely comfortable with this outcome. You will detect the note of self-congratulation in my account of myself. I am aware of it, but I'm not sure what to do about it. Should I deny my feelings? A friend of mine on the West Coast recently wrote me that after two years of trying to adjust to having diabetes and to establish himself in his career at the same time, he had come out whole and modestly successful, and he was greatly pleased. Those who love the man can only be pleased for him. He earned it, didn't he? We turn guilty too quickly, I think, when we consider our circumstances and our successes and pronounce them good. I know I react this way; some part of me is sure I'm ripe for tragedy, that whatever success I have and whatever pleasure I take in it will be taken away. I don't really deserve it, I tell myself.

It becomes practically a fixed sequence: you arrive at a goal and that makes you happy, but then you notice that the happiness is composed half of relief, half of self-satisfaction; the latter half makes you distinctly nervous, and you fall to chewing on your achievements, discounting them. This then becomes the spur to more achievements, more happiness, more guilt. How much better, I sometimes think, to have no goals, just to live day by day. Would I be happy then? No, my mother's ghost wouldn't allow it. Life is hard, she told me; life is a struggle. So I struggle happily on, running through the sequence again and again, fighting off the impulse to pat myself on the back but remaining, like my friend, fundamentally pleased. That's the American way, isn't it? My contempt for the pursuit of happiness is a joke. I'm playing this game as hard as the next fellow.

But I have doubts. There are plenty of ways besides the American way. We Americans identify the pursuit of happiness with the pursuit of success, money, achievement; we think we'll be happy when we make it, although we love to believe that those who do make it are actually quite miserable. But I think of my father, who seemed to have no ambition, perfectly content, as far as I could tell, to work in the same job for the same company for thirty-five years, to come home to his wife and children every single night, read the paper, eat dinner, never go anywhere but to our cottage at the shore for two weeks and weekends during the summer. My father was intelligent and talented; he had a beautiful singing voice, he could draw with great accuracy, but he made no effort to develop any of his talents. An assistant manager for twenty years, he had no desire to become manager. It used to drive my mother crazy; she was ambitious for him, she wanted him to push. He was immovable. When he retired, he spent the next ten years puttering around in his garden, which he never finished, and doing crossword puzzles. Still driving my mother crazy. I used to think he had wasted his life. Arrogant of me. I remember visiting him in his office and always finding him having a good time, chatting with his fellow workers, the very image of a happy man. Was this wasteful?

My brother and I are both driven workaholics; my father lived in an entirely different framework. I think of the Greeks in connection with him; their idea of a happy life was a life led outside history, a quiet life like his. Their archetypal illustration was the story Herodotus tells about the lawgiver Solon's conversation with the Lydian king Croesus, who was legendary for his wealth. Solon, who was legendary for his widsom, was on a ten-year tour of the known world when he met Croesus, who showed him his treasury and then asked him who he thought was the happiest of all the men he had met. Croesus believed, of course, that being the richest he would certainly have to be the happiest. Solon rapidly set him straight. Who is a happy man? He who "is whole of limb," Solon replied, "a stranger to disease, free from misfortune, happy in his children, and comely to look upon." No more is necessary, except that he die well.

All of this was true of my father. He had enough money; he was whole of limb; he was almost never sick; he loved his children; he was even relatively good-looking. And he died well. The only time he ever spent in a hospital was the last four days of his life; he had a heart attack, spent four days in intensive care, and then, as quietly as he had lived, died. Here was happiness, not pursued but possessed anyhow.

Then there's the price those of us like his two sons pay, and force others to, for our obsession with this will-o'-the-wisp, happiness. A woman I hoped to marry wanted me to give up free-lance writing and get a job in public relations. I was making about six thousand dollars a year at the time and living on my dreams and my MasterCard. We had nothing. It was clear to both of us that we could hardly make a decent life together if my prospects didn't rapidly improve. And I might have made forty thousand dollars a year in PR. I flirted with the idea, saw some people, but nothing came of it. No one will hire me, I told her. You didn't really try, she replied. What do you mean? I said, indignant; of course I did. Of course I didn't. The truth I didn't want to admit to her, or to myself, was that I loved the work I was doing more than I loved her. She left eventually, and I was glad to see her go. I wanted the guilt she represented out of my life.

We can be selfish and ruthless in the pursuit of happiness, make choices other people have to live and suffer with, and there's no guarantee that it's going to work out. The odds are, in fact, that we won't make it, whatever "it" is, that the losses will outweigh the gains. The odds are what's keeping my friend Paul, who desperately wants to change his life, from doing it. Paul is thirty-five, married, and has an eleven-year-old son. He works as an advertising copywriter and does well, but what he really wants is to go back to graduate school, get his Ph.D. in English literature, then get a teaching job and write fiction on the side. But to do all this would mean selling his house, asking his wife to go to work, and using the savings he has accumulated for his son's education for his own. He tells me that he sometimes spends hours figuring out exactly what he would need, how much the house would bring, how much his wife might make if she got a job, and what his chances are of getting a job in the overcrowded market for Ph.D.s. But no matter how carefully he draws up this budget—the figures, he says, are a simulacrum of his loyalties—there's never enough money.

The risks involved in such a choice are enormous, and Paul is at heart not ruthless or selfish enough to take them. If he were alone, he says, sure. And he says his wife is willing to stand behind him whatever he decides. But he can't do it, and this seems in most respects admirable; it was apparently my father's choice, it is the Greek choice, the choice to be content with one's lot and not ask too many sacrifices from other people in the service of something so insubstantial, so vague, as a possibility of happiness beyond what one already has. And yet Paul is not a happy man. He is not ruthless or selfish, no, but he sees this as a lack of courage, a failure to believe in his own talent; he calls himself a coward.

I understand Paul and I know what he's going through. I made my choice a long time ago, but it took me a long time to make it. And when I did, it cost me everything I owned, and it cost my ex-wife and my two kids and later my fiancée, not to mention assorted friends and relatives, one hell of a lot of pain. And for what? For an old bitch gone in the teeth, to reapply Pound's metaphor to my own success, such as it is. I am proud of the work I've done, proud of staying with it when the reward was only six thousand dollars a year and my hair was already starting to turn gray; but I'm not proud of my own ruthlessness and selfishness and I wish I had had it in me to be more like my father.

The pursuit of happiness was serious business to Jefferson, but his idea of happiness, as I mentioned at the beginning, was quite different from ours. Happiness at the time of the Declaration was not a state of mind that one pursued in and for oneself but a version of the common good, an idea of general human felicity that one pursued both for oneself and for all. Jefferson was trying to establish the idea that government has no right to stand in the way of our pursuit of felicity so conceived. The form that felicity took for Jefferson was a society composed very much along the Greek model, with lots of farmers living quiet lives, practicing quiet virtues, making money but not too much, and reading Herodotus by candlelight.

It hasn't turned out that way. We have identified happiness with success and we are stuck with it now, so that people like my father seem like washouts to people like my mother and the only happiness I can find is in the struggle to succeed. I suppose it couldn't have happened otherwise. But I am tempted to cry, Enough! To rest easy with what I have, finish reading Herodotus and then move on to Plutarch, perhaps take up crossword puzzles, leave pursuits to others. A gentleman farmer. It was wise of my father not to finish his garden, for he would only have had to start another. Now he's gone, I missed the message of his life, I have condemned myself to this pursuit. Oh, I love it, make no mistake, but the pursuit of happiness feels to me sometimes like a dog chasing its tail and half of me thinks that we have made a giant mistake, that the American way is little more than the exaltation of greed.

Thought

1. Why does the author assert, "Life has always seemed to me a testing ground"?
2. According to Brandt, what is the natural outcome of achievement?
3. How does the author's understanding of happiness differ from his father's?
4. Which of these views of happiness is closer to your own view? Explain.

5.   Do you agree that one can be "selfish and ruthless in the pursuit of happiness"? Justify your opinion.
6.   a) Is Brandt justified in asserting that "the American way is little more than the exaltation of greed"?
     b) Is this the Canadian view also?

Style and Structure

7.   Examine several anecdotes upon which Brandt reflects. Determine which anecdotes are illustrative and which are developmental.
8.   What stylistic purposes are served by Brandt's references to Jefferson?

Response and Extension

9.   For discussion: To what extent are selfishness and the pursuit of happiness synonymous?
10. Interview someone whom you consider to be happy. Write an essay in which you reflect upon why that person is happy.
11. In your journal, reflect upon what makes you happy.

Some Thoughts on the Cute, Cute Fifties

Anne Rivers Siddons

- Discuss the importance of peer pressure in your life in terms of behaviour, dress, language and attitudes.
- Look up the etymology of the word "cute." List and discuss several modern connotations of "cute."

This past April, gritting my teeth through the spell of Cleaning Up that shakes me annually like a demon terrier, I came upon a cardboard box in the attic that held my high school cheerleader's uniform. It was carefully tissue-wrapped and moth-balled, undoubtedly the work of my mother, who tends to preserve my castoff ceremonial garments as though they will be donated to a museum one day. I lifted it out; a yellowed white V-necked sweater with a monumental blue C on the front; a hideous, ankle-flapping corduroy skirt of alternating blue and white gores, satin-lined; a pinheaded blue felt beanie; blue satin tights gone brittle and frayed with age. There was a spreading reddish stain across that skirt that came, I remembered, from sprawling headlong into a sea of red mud at the apex of an abortive cartwheel one Friday evening. The sweater had a darker, rusty stain that was the stigmata of some long-forgotten hero's nosebleed when I hugged him after a victory. Even the socks—the long, thick ones you rolled down into salami-like cuffs around your ankles, just above the bump-toed saddle oxfords— were there. Brushing attic dust and warm, fond, sycophantic tears off my face, I took off my Levis and sweat shirt and put them all on.

Creeping downstairs like a shy shade afraid to haunt my own house, I padded shoeless to my bedroom mirror. It gave me back a figure from a Poe masque. Swatched and shrouded in dingy, too-long corduroy and too-bulky white wool, a true specter looked back at me with frank fright. The uniform still fit, but the blank, stone-smooth, black-lipsticked young face that belonged above it, framed with a slicked-back duck-tail, had been replaced with a face that belonged above tweed and turtleneck at the supermarket. It was grotesque, like a baby in a sequined jumpsuit, or a matron in a romper. "Sis-boom-bah," I whispered carefully to the image, doing as if by rote a viscerally-remembered pirouette that showed a flash of shredding blue tights. *That* was truly terrifying, and I dashed into the den, where my husband was watching Howard Cosell, for succor.

By all rights, he should have laughed, but he didn't. He smiled and hugged me and said, "You look sweet. I'll bet you were a cute teen-ager."

Looking back, I realize that's just what I was. It was what we all were in the mid-fifties, we Revloned and duck-or-ponytailed young girls; were, or aspired to be. Cute. The word may sum up that generation of naïve nubility better than any word has ever evoked the young-female-ness of any age.

Not for any of us the beckoning comets of professional eminence, political influence, or even what the Victorians called "a brilliant marriage." Marriage, certainly, was the carrot that motivated the young donkeys, but the prospects of a brilliant one would have terrified us. Uniform anonymity was our Grail. There was not a fledgling Curie or Bernhardt among us, not a De Staël-to-be, not a cadet Stein, not an aspiring Great Beauty or even a magnificent courtesan. The natural, healthy amorality of the female young was buffed out of existence by the etiquette column in *Seventeen* magazine. Any hint of sensuality was instinctively sublimated into such strictured physical channels as the girls' basketball team, the drill squad, the majorette corps. And, of course, the cheerleading team. We necked, naturally, in a succession of our fathers' Chevvies out behind the gym after sock hops, or on Bluebird buses coming home from out-of-town football games, but it was more ritual than ripening, and about as sexy as the matings of oysters. Even physical desirability had to be ersatz to be acceptable. A burgeoning bosom—a *real* one—was armored away beneath starched dickies. (Conversely, it was proper, if one was bosomless, to correct the oversight with dreadful, concentrically stitched affairs known as Peter Pan bras, as rigid and uniformly molded as those silver bullet-shaped projectiles on the bumpers of '51 Studebakers. Why this was okay and real breasts vaguely shameful I can't recall. Presumably, an impressive cantilever was fine so long as it didn't jiggle.)

A pair of really fine, delicately hollowed cheekbones or a high-bridged roman nose were afflictions second only to acne. To be tall was to be unclean. It was the era of the button-nosed, squirrel-cheeked, dimpled Cute Face. God, what we wouldn't suffer in the name of Cutehood.

An ordinary spring school day was a case in point. My peers and I would get up at dawn for the rites of hairdressing. I to untorture the million tiny pin curls with which I tried—vainly—to subdue my thick, curly mop into a sculptured, fluff-fringed, side-banged cap; they to create helmet-smooth pageboys, perfect poodle cuts, or enameled pony-tails with a rubberized circlet of artificial flowers where the tail met the pony. The nylon panties came next, and the ubiquitous, stabbing Peter Pans, then a layered assemblage of crinolines in various stages of flaccidity. After that, a starched sleeveless blouse with a high, military collar, centered by another clump of artificial flora, or a scarf. Over that went, almost to a maiden, a chain bearing an outsized class ring. A starched circle of skirt next; we had permanent abrasions at midcalf where all that starch and crinoline met leg. An elasticized cinch belt finished off the whole ensemble and often the wearer; our high school Phys. Ed. teacher once made an impassioned appeal in Friday morning assembly for this elastic foolishness to cease, since hyperventilating young ladies were passing out like flies in unair-conditioned halls and homerooms.

Then, in pinched bare feet, black kid Capezio shell slippers or pleated-toe ballet slippers. And on to make-up.

I can still remember the *maquillage* of the fifties. It was as formal and prescribed as a Kabuki dancer's. First a coat of Helena Rubinstein in Rachel. Then polka dots of Cuticura to mask the hickies. Then a flouring of Rachel powder that stayed Rachel only until you worked up the day's first sweat, at which point it turned orange. Vivid, primary green or blue half-moons of eye shadow, if your parents permitted it. Black Maybelline mascara put on with spit and a brush. Black Maybelline eyebrow pencil. And finally, a thick paste of Fire and Ice lipstick if you were brunette, Persian Melon if anything else. And a cloying squirt of Fabergé—Woodhue or Tigress—to mingle with all the Mum and Odor-O-No creams rising steamily from stinging young armpits in homerooms. Small wonder windows were kept open; wonder, indeed, that this icing of drugstore Vilma Banky could be considered Cute. But it was.

In fall and winter, the make-up stayed constant, but the uniform changed. Hobbling wool skirts with a rakish, two-inch side slit to display the obligatory lace slip. Matched twin sets—cashmere if you were well born, lamb's wool if you were not, quite; nylon given to rabbitlike pilling if you were below the salt. Starched white Peter Pan collars that fit under your sweater neck and produced another, garrotelike abrasion, or a single strand of pearls that came exactly to your collarbone. The ring-on-a-chain or, in some sophisticated instances, a college fraternity pin posed dizzily on the left Peter Pan extrusion. The fat-sausage socks (angora, one miserable, itching year), and Bass Weejuns with a penny in them. It didn't much matter about your winter coat; if you were Popular, you wore some young Clydesdale's letter jacket, and if you weren't, no one really cared if you froze. Least of all you.

Prom nights were occasions for exquisite, Torquemada-like torture. I don't know about the rest of the country, but in the South, we wore, by God, hoop skirts. They came in a round plastic box about the size of a cake tin and consisted of three tiers of graduated, expansible rings, which, when fully flowered, looked something like the superstructure of a surrealistic Christmas tree. These came next to last, however, just before your formal. First there was a three-hour celebration of bathing, oiling, shaving, talcuming, buffing, perfuming, currying, combing out, and the inevitable Make-up. This was rendered prom-worthy by the addition of tarnished-gold or pewtery eye shadow and an extra helping of Fire and Ice, which would bleed gorily onto several rental tuxedo lapels by the end of the first "slow dance." Then lace-trimmed, Christmas-present panties, and slick, opaque stockings weeping ankle-ward from garter belts. (Frightful things, these, but I am assured by several men of my current acquaintance that those strapped and buckled devices were, and still are, the sexiest undergarment ever donned by women.) Then a truly terrible thing called a Merry Widow, another Peter Pan contrivance which came to midhip, pushed your bosom skyward (often augmented by another pair of stockings, to produce a chaste, linear cleavage), and required the services of your mother and your best friend to snap up the back. The legendary waists of the antebellum South had been hardened into young tree trunks in the fifties by field hockey and physical education, but at least twice a year they dwindled to near-Scarlett diameter.

Over this armadillo-like carapace went the hoop, extended into its full, *bibelot*-smashing circumference, and then the formal. Boned and strapless they were, of net or tulle, with acres of drifting skirts, often sprinkled with sequins or rhinestones, and they were infallibly pink, blue, mint green, yellow, or lavender. A net stole went along with most, as did dangling rhinestone earrings, a beaded evening bag, which would hold compact and lipstick but not your illicit Pall Malls, a velvet or bunny-fur jacket or your mother's fur stole. And silver or gold ballet slippers, since most of us were as tall as our dates.

You would clank like a pastel tank into your living room, unable to sit, propped against a handy mantel, until your date, unhappy and alien in tux and dangling, red-wristed hands and Vaseline Hair Tonic, arrived bearing a purple orchid or a funereal white posy of carnations. And then began the *opéra bouffe* of getting you into his father's car.

We double-dated then, by necessity, since few of our gentlemen callers had cars of their own, and those who did owned malodorous hot rods bared to the elements and entirely unsuitable for conveying a cargo of elephantine butterflies. One couple would already be in the back seat, he cowering against the door, she peering from an auto-filling, overrisen soufflé of skirt which her hoops had pushed up around her shoulders. I forget the precise technique for getting into a car in a hoop skirt, but it involved raising the whole affair to waist level behind and sidling in sidewise. You would not, of course, expose your behind to your date, so you shone your panties toward your own front door. I have more than once heard my treacherous father chuckling as I departed for a prom.

My musings on the Cute, Cute Fifties did not include, this spring, any thought as to the wherefores of them. It was, to me, a strange, muffled, frightened, smug time, perhaps more so in the South. Somehow the tenor of every age seems to be intensified into caricature in the South. I don't remember having a very good time during the fifties, though I certainly thought I was at the time. Perhaps it was because, in the core of my soul, I never achieved true Cutehood, though I did the walk-through faultlessly.

I leave the tenor of those times to Peter Bogdanovitch and Dan Greenburg, who have caught them exquisitely, though, as Dylan Thomas said wistfully of the wasp book he received on one of his legendary Christmases in Wales, they told me everything I wished to know about the fifties except why.

But the powerful magic of Cutehood lingers on. It must. Recently, a friend gave a costume party. And seven women came in their high school cheerleaders' uniforms.

Thought

1. What aspects of the fifties as reflected upon by Siddons are similar to your own experiences?

2. Which aspects of the fifties as articulated in this essay do you find most foreign to your experience?

Style and Structure

3. List five words or phrases which best describe the adolescent fashion of the period. List five words that you would use to describe the adolescent fashion of today. Compare your two lists.
4. Does this essay have a clearly defined thesis? Explain.
5. Analyse the author's attitude toward her subject by quoting specific sentences from the essay.
6. Identify the audience that you think Siddons had in mind when she was writing this reflective essay.

Response and Extension

7. Write a reflective essay entitled "Adolescence: Uniform Anonymity."
8. Write an essay or a short story about a school-related social occasion.

On Hating Piano Lessons

Phyllis Theroux

> - What things do your parents insist you do because "they are good for you"?
> - Should parents insist that their children do things which are "good for them"?

When I was growing up, I conceived of children as being of two kinds: those who took lessons and those who did not. I was the second kind, although I sometimes accompanied my horseback-riding, accordion-playing, baton-twirling friends to their classes and, by osmosis, learned a few things that enabled me to fake an expertise in a crowd. But with one exception I was self-taught, flinging my arms and legs around the living room doing badly executed *tours jetés* to Gilbert and Sullivan records, which allowed me to assume all the parts and, on one occasion, to break my ankle. I did, however, take piano lessons.

Once I discovered the sound that three fingers simultaneously placed on the right keys could produce, I longed so loudly and consistently for piano lessons that my mother began to think maybe I was a genius and she did not want to go to her grave thinking I had become a short-order cook for want of an option. Options, in the long run, are what lessons are all about.

Now I am a parent. I think about giving my children options and lessons, although children don't understand that their once-a-week session with Madame Faustini at the keyboard cancels out their mother's once-a-month visit to "The Magic Scissors." But hair-cuts play second fiddle to Beethoven if I am financially solvent, and this year my ten-year-old daughter is taking piano lessons—under duress.

My daughter does not like piano lessons. They are too hard. Her teacher, a wild and dedicated woman who drives around in a yellow convertible and annually volunteers to sit on the "Dunk-'Em" chair at the school bazaar, understands about ten-year-old girls who would rather be talking on the telephone, and she always tries to give her pieces to learn that are on the jazzy side. But my daughter, though dutiful, has not been won over by this enlightened approach. Furthermore, she claims, her heart lies with gymnastics, a message I bought last year, along with a leotard which now lies neglected in her bottom bureau drawer.

When she was halfway through gymnastics, her heart began to rove down the hall toward a tap-dancing class that sounded a lot better to her ears. I canceled gymnastics and enrolled her in tap, wanting to stake this small developing plant, my daughter, with the kinds of support that would strengthen and develop her soul.

Unfortunately, her soul turned out to be a shifting, shiftless creature, and her interest in tap dancing waned after the sixth lesson. Suddenly, she saw pottery (which happened to have a class in the same building) as the wave of her future. But tiring of always chasing cultural advantages that were in another room, I decided that what my daughter wanted was immaterial. I wanted her to take piano lessons.

At the beginning, all was well. But when she had gone through the honeymoon period of her first few lessons and realized there was more to it than pasting gold stars in new music books, gymnastics began to appeal to her anew. This time, however, I looked her straight in the eye and said, unflinchingly, "This year it's piano lessons. In fact, next year it's piano lessons, too, unless I can't afford them." It seemed important to let her know that there was no way out.

My daughter thinks I am cruel, that I don't understand her, that I am trying to force her to be something she is not. My daughter is right. I want her, when she is thirty-five or sixty and feeling temporarily low on being, to be able to converse with Mozart, call up Clementi, or have a romp with Rodgers and Hammerstein at *will*, which is what lessons of any kind develop the capacity to use.

This is a difficult wish to communicate to a child who looks at me with "don't make me do it" eyes when I drop her off for a lesson where she must spend another hour forcing her mind and fingers up and down the G and treble clefts. But I have hardened myself to her accusatory looks, and while my daughter has her reasons for complaint, my old heart has its reasons for making her suffer which her heart, being young, cannot fully understand.

There will come a time, I think, as I watch you trudge up the steps to your teacher's house, when your heart will be empty. There will come a time when words, no matter how many or how eloquent, will do you no good at all. There will come a time when no one thing or person can adequately express the soul inside you that needs to be articulated. And then, my gymnastic, tap-dancing daughter, if I have been sufficiently "cruel" to you, you will have music.

But Time divides us at this moment. There are some things one cannot explain to a ten-year-old girl who is only in Book One of piano and life. I must adjust myself to being the mean parent who doesn't understand, and perhaps I don't. Perhaps my daughter *is* a gymnast, or a tap dancer, or the world's number one potter who, when she is grown, will rightly accuse me of having thrown her on the wrong wheel. But in the meantime, in-between time, she is taking piano lessons.

Thought

1. Identify the main idea, or thesis, of the essay.
2. According to the writer, what purpose do lessons serve? Do you agree with her?
3. Why does Theroux decide that "What my daughter wanted was immaterial"? Is she justified in this decision?

Style and Structure

4. Indicate the shifts in focus which Theroux uses to structure her essay. What purposes are served by those shifts in focus?
5. Demonstrate that Theroux uses humour effectively to emphasize her thesis.

Response and Extension

6. Write an essay reflecting upon a sport or activity you were forced to participate in as a child. Be sure to include both your feelings about the situation then and your feelings about it now.
7. Write a letter to your parent or guardian explaining why you will not do something he or she wants you to do.

The Rear-View Mirror: Notes Toward a Future

Northrop Frye

- What are the purposes of a university?
- What distinguishes the humanities from the sciences?

I have been called, very generously, a scholar, and ideally there is no difference between a scholar and a teacher. But in practice there is a good deal of difference, at least in emphasis. I think all my books have been teaching books rather than scholarly books: I keep reformulating the same central questions, trying to put them into a form to which some reader or student will respond: "Yes, now I get it." A more typical scholar than I, I should think, can be much more of a guru: he can train other scholars; he is at his best in the graduate school, and when his students become scholars in their turn, they have his brand mark, so to speak, printed on them. I teach mainly undergraduates, and I find the undergraduate classroom important for my writing. And yet the teacher-student relation, as such, seems to me a curiously embarrassing one: I want my students released from it as soon as possible to go and do their own thing. Their own thing may very well be teaching, of course; but what interests me even more is the great variety of things that students in an undergraduate classroom go on to do. Because this is what indicates most clearly the variety of ways that the university affects the society it belongs to.

I recently read an article, written by someone much younger than myself, which said sternly that the twentieth century is moving so fast that anyone born when I was, in 1912, is at best a survivor from an earlier age, a dinosaur who may not realize how cold it's getting. But it has been often pointed out that Canada itself is peculiarly a land of survival: a huge loosely assembled collection of territories, divided by language, geography and politics, can only stay together by constantly meeting a series of crises, each of them carrying the threat of not surviving if the crisis is not met. So perhaps Canada has something in common with my generation. During the sixty-odd years that Canada and I have survived together, it seems to me that Canada has become steadily more typical of the world it is in. Survival in itself is nothing to be complacent about: people survive a war only because other people do not; and if we worry less about nuclear destruction than we did, it is because the worry is intolerable, not because the threat is any less of a threat. But the survival of society as a whole is usually considered a good thing: we may be surviving in a fool's paradise, but perhaps no other paradise is appropriate for human beings.

If I can believe what that article said, along with so many others that say much the same thing, the world I was born into in 1912 was both a stable world and a simple one, a world of ordered values, whereas now these values are being questioned or denied, and are either disappearing or turning into something else. People of my generation, in short, were brought up to be against sin and in favour of motherhood, and can't cope with a world where motherhood is out and sin is in. Being a literary critic, when I am faced with statements like this I look first at the literary conventions behind them, and then at the metaphors they use. The convention is what critics call a pastoral myth, and it descends from ancient stories of lost gardens of Eden and vanished golden ages. Pastoral myths are mostly illusions projected from the experience of growing older. A child's world seems simple and innocent to the adult, so he assumes that the world as a whole was simpler when he was a child, and by extension even simpler before that. But however natural this assumption may be it is clearly nonsense: there have never been any simple ages.

As for the metaphors, what they really say is: the world used to be solid; now it's liquid. The basis for these metaphors is chiefly money; if we can put a dollar into a bank with a reasonable hope of still having a dollar when we take it out again, then our world looks solid, and all our social, political and religious values look solid too. Rapid inflation makes the world liquidate very quickly, and we have to live from one moment to the next by a combination of faith and self-hypnotism, like the people in the Far East who walk over hot coals, to the great bewilderment of tourists, most of whom are capable of self-hypnotism but not of faith.

What I am talking about is what is often called future shock, the sense of uneasiness caused by a technology moving faster than the human ability to control it. This is also a standard myth, the story of the sorcerer's apprentice, the machine that could be started but not stopped.

Uneasiness about the future is there, certainly, and the basis for it is real enough; but I have no expertise in this area. What I hope I do know something about starts with the fact that there is no such thing as future shock, because nobody knows one instant of the future, except by analogy with the past.

Metaphors are tricky things to handle. We think we know that the earth revolves around the sun, but we still say "sunrise" and "sunset" because we don't really believe it. The sun revolves around the world that concerns us, and doubtless always will. Similarly, if we're driving a car, we look ahead of us to see where we're going, but what applies to moving in space doesn't apply to moving in time. We move in time with our backs to what's ahead and our faces to the past, and all we know is in a rear-view mirror. But we don't like to think this way: we say to a young person: "you have a great future ahead of you", and forget what we mean is: "you will probably have a good deal more past to contemplate". The humanities are often reproached with their concern over the past, but there is no difference between the humanities and any other form of knowledge on this point. The humanities change just as radically as the sciences do, and on the same principles. There is nothing new under the sun except our knowledge of what is under the sun, but that new knowledge is a constant recreation of old knowledge.

The question "Where are we going?" assumes that we already know the answer to the question "Where are we now, and how did we get here?" We certainly don't know the answer to that one, and in fact all our really urgent, mysterious and frightening questions have to do with the burden of the past and the meaning of tradition. Here we are in Canada, confronted with so many problems that demand immediate solution. Nobody denies their importance, but what continues to fascinate us is the reinterpreting of our history. What seems really important to us is that all Canadians don't agree with the British North America Act of a century ago, or about the Quebec Act a century before that. Oh well, we say, that's just Canada, always fussing about its identity, like a neurotic who can't deal with the world until he's got his private past unsnarled. But it isn't just Canada: there's the weight of a past of slavery on emerging nations in Africa, the weight of the British Empire on contemporary Britain, of the Old Testament on Israel, of Marxist doctrine on the Soviet Union. Up to the Vietnam war, more or less, many people in the United States believed that the American way of life had only to progress and look ahead: their view of life for themselves was based on the car-driving metaphor. But now most Americans also, I think, regard their past as something in front of them to be studied, not behind them to run away from.

I understand the fear that our civilization will fail to adapt in time to the changes which its technology has already started. But the word "adapt" may be misleading, because there is no environment to adapt to except the one we have created. Man is the one animal that has stopped playing the Darwinian game of adaptation, and has tried to transform the environment instead. Much of his transformation so far has been pollution, waste, overcrowding and destruction, and there is a limit beyond which he can't go on doing this. At least I hope there's a limit: there are movies like *Star Wars* which suggest that we can learn to visit distant galaxies and smash them up too; but I'd prefer not to think of that as our future.

The American poet Wallace Stevens wrote a poem called "Description Without Place," in which he says that man does not live directly in the world, he lives inside his own constructs of that world. Nothing like nationality has any existence in nature, and yet, Stevens says, when we are in Spain everything looks Spanish. A parallel of latitude divides Canada from the United States; a meridian of longitude, Manitoba from Saskatachewan. Such things don't exist in the world of birds and trees, of course; but on the other hand, the world of birds and trees doesn't exist for us, except as part of the constructed human world which starts with things like Canada and its provinces.

I have spent most of my professional life studying one aspect of the way man constructs the world he lives in; the aspect I call a mythology, the building of worlds out of words. Nobody can create, think or even act outside the mythology of his time, but a mythology is not some kind of prison; it is simply the whole body of verbal material we work with. Like science, it is being recreated all the time, partly by critics and scholars and partly by literature itself, because every new writer recreates something already in literature. So anyone teaching literature gets involved with mythology, and this very quickly carries him past the boundaries of literature into the social function of words.

In forty years of teaching, I have never seen any differences among my students, as students, that could be ascribed to sex or ethnical origin. But of course I see any amount of social conditioning, in every classroom I go into. Gradually it dawns on a teacher of English that he is in contact with the student's total verbal experience, and that probably less than one per cent of that experience has been derived from anything that he would call literature. The rest is made up of social conditioning, from television and other news media, casual conversations, advertising, the chattering of the student's own subconscious, and so on. All teachers know that their students need to become aware of and question their assumptions; but perhaps the teacher of English sees most clearly how militant a job teaching is, and what kind of enemy it has to fight. What faces him is not simply a mass of unexamined assumptions but a complete and mostly phony mythology, made up of cliché and prejudice and stock response, a kind of parody of the one he is trying to teach.

We think of reading as essential to living in a modern society, which of course it is. But in itself it only attaches us to that society; it doesn't set us free from it. In the subway, where I do a certain amount of my writing, I can see around me four signs telling me not to do things, three sets of instructions about what to do in an emergency, and two threats of fine or imprisonment if there turns out not to be any emergency. There is also a long document in fine print I have never read, besides all the advertising. It's clear that the primary motive for teaching one to read is to produce an obedient and adjusted citizen, who can respond to a traffic sign with the right reflex. This conformity is probably the only basis for living in a complicated society: we belong to something before we are anything, and the individual grows out of the group, not the other way round. There is nothing much wrong with the fact that most students are conformists, including of course the rebellious students, who are bigoted conformists. But social adjustment is a beginning, not an end, and on this basis of conformity the teacher has to work for their liberal education, trying to transfer their loyalties from ready-made responses to the real world of human constructive power. As the university comes very late in a student's life, the teacher may have to work only with a few, but that few makes all the difference in the level of the civilization it belongs to.

How is it that people get trapped in phony mythologies? As Thomas Pynchon says in his novel *Gravity's Rainbow*, man is a paranoid animal, always claiming that the world he's made is the real world, and that it's the order of God or of nature, or both, as well. This means, in reverse, that there can't be any reality that doesn't have an essential relation to us. The notion that God made the world primarily for the sake of man was built into our religious consciousness for centuries. What other point could there possibly be in making the world? people asked, without realizing how sick their question was. It was a slow and painful adjustment to seeing the world as a place that got along for millions of years without man, and still could, in fact still may. Or else we claim that what we impose on our world is what nature put there. When we had a society with "nobles" on top and "commoners" below, people tended to assume that those on top had "noble blood," and were better by birth or nature than the others.

Such constructs are at first partial: in early times one nation would assume that it had supreme rights over the rest of the world; another nation would make the same assumption, so they would go to war, and the winner was the one who was right. But as human life has slowly expanded over the whole globe, it has become steadily clearer that all enemies, proletariats, slaves, scapegoats and second-class people are products of illusion, things to be outgrown, and the longer we cling to such illusions, the more obviously evil and disastrous our attachment to them becomes. St. Paul reminded the Athenians that there is only one human race: I say reminded, because he clearly assumed that it was a fact they would know. We know it too, but are very unwilling to act on it: however, there are signs that we are making a beginning. Some of us have even begun to wonder whether the world of animals and plants, perhaps also of coal and oil deposits, really exists only for our benefit.

Every classroom shows a division between those who take in what education is about and those who stay with cliché and stock response. This creates a distinction that I would call the distinction between concern and anxiety. Concern is the response of the adult citizen to genuine social problems. Anxiety is based on the desire to exclude or subordinate, to preserve the values or benefits of society for the group of right people who know the right answers. The anxieties closest to teaching the humanities, I suppose, are those of prudery and propriety, or what I think of as garrison anxieties, the desire to keep everyone in parade uniform so that it will be easy to distinguish the officers.

One of the more attractive features of my own life in Toronto has been in seeing many anxieties of this type gradually relaxed, or even abandoned. In my younger days there was a great deal of anxious deference paid to women, of a kind that was clearly connected with keeping them out of many fields of social activity. There were anxieties about the freedom of expression claimed by painters and sculptors, and art galleries resounded with comparisons to what one's five-year-old kid could do. There were frantic anxieties about sexual scenes or four-letter words in books: the copy of *Ulysses* that I am still using was smuggled in to me from Buffalo by a friend. When I was a student, a young woman in a Latin class who had memorized the crib went on placidly translating a passage of Horace which the anxious editor had removed from the text to safeguard her purity, and I have never forgotten the vision of futility that that opened up for me. Religious bodies cultivated special kinds of anxiety, and felt that it increased their virtue to do so. Jokes that assumed racial or sexual or class prejudice abounded, and the assumptions in them were more or less taken for granted. And a policewoman set up as a sexual decoy could hardly be festooned with more warnings and special instructions than those surrounding the purchase of liquor.

Nevertheless, Toronto went on expanding from an uptight Scotch-

Irish town to a cosmopolitan city, with art galleries and theatres and bookshops presenting a kind of imaginative experience that fifty years ago would have filled the newspapers with screams of panic and despair. I know that all this is only a normal part of a big city's growth; I am merely saying that it has been rather exhilarating to live through. I know too that no dragon ever dies: many people feel that their security is bound up with their anxieties, and Canadian novelists even yet are struggling with the same kind of hysteria that faced Morley Callaghan half a century ago. It may be thought too that many of these things are rather trivial. I happen not to think so. It's the job of a teacher of the humanities to keep fighting for the liberalizing of the imagination, to encourage students to confront experience, to explore the shadows and the darkness, to distinguish evil from the portrayal of evil, and to meet the unexpected with tolerance. If I am right, this is a fight on the front line of social good will, an aspect of what in religion is called charity.

The democratic ideal is one of equality, where everyone has the same rights before the law, but not, except indirectly, one of freedom. It tries to provide the conditions of freedom, but freedom itself is an experience, not a condition, and only the individual can experience it. So for freedom there has to be some tension between society and the individual. As the democracies have continued to maintain this tension, another movement has begun to take shape, which I think may be the most significant social movement of our time. This is the rise of the small community that coheres around a cultural tradition. For culture, in contrast to political and economic movements, tends to decentralize: it is usually based on a distinctive language, which is one of the most fragmented forms of human expression, and its products, like fine wines, are restricted to a small area in growth, if not in appeal.

In the world around us there are, first, the colonies of the old empires which have come to independence, and are now looking for their own cultural traditions. Then there are the small ethnic groups that have refused to be entirely assimilated to larger ones, like the Welsh in Britain or the Bretons in France. Some of these groups have a long history of oppression and repression, and partly because of this they may include violent or terroristic elements. These are naturally the ones we get to hear most about, but they are not the really significant ones, because violence always brings about the opposite of what it aims at. The extent to which political separation may be necessary for a culture will vary with circumstances, and often it may be simply the result of clinging to obsolete patterns of thinking. The centralizing political and economic movements have built up huge cities; these cities are now almost unmanageable, and I think a decentralizing cultural movement is likely to become more dominant. But I think as it goes on it will also become less political.

In every part of Canada there are strong separatist feelings, some political, as in Quebec, some economic, as in the west, some geographical, as in the Maritimes. But the genuine movement underlying all this is a feeling of cultural distinctiveness, and this, I think, will keep breaking down into smaller units as more of the country becomes articulate. In the last fifteen years or so, I have noticed how an increasing number of writers and painters in Canada have come to regard the place where they are living not as an accident, but as an environment that nourishes them, and which they in turn bring into articulateness. We speak of American literature, but what we have are mainly Mississippi writers, New England writers, Parisian expatriate writers, southern California writers. Similarly, I think Canadian literature will become more and more a literature of regions. It seems to be a cultural law that the more specific the setting of literature is, the more universal its communicating power.

One reason why this movement interests me is that it could give the university a social function which would be its traditional function renewed. The reason why I have stayed in the university is very largely the fact that I have never got over the impact of my four undergraduate years. As an undergraduate, I was in a small community of students concerned mainly with the liberal arts. This was a community in which life could be experienced with a far greater intensity than anywhere else, because it was a life in which the intellect and the imagination had a functional role to play. It is no good arguing with me, or with anyone else who has had a similar experience, about the practical value of spending four years at university. The experience is its own value, and is a totally irreplaceable one. Modern universities have been geared to political and economic expansion: they have developed into multiversities, with research institutes and professional training centres. As a result systems of financing have grown up that are based on size, and have practically compelled the universities to compete for students and to suggest that degrees were essential for a better job or social position. We still need research institutes and professional training schools: the question is whether they should be set up in such a way as to smother one of the real centres of university life. I would hope to see the small university community come into focus again as the spark plug of a small cultural area that was beginning to feel its own articulateness.

I began by saying that the rear-view mirror is our only crystal ball: there is no guide to the future except the analogy of the past. But one's view of the past is coloured by prejudice and narrowed by ignorance, and so the future, when it comes to join the past, is always unexpected. Many people base their lives on what they think of as the future: the writer hopes he will be read in the future if he is neglected at present; the radical dreams of a revolutionary future and the conservative of a safeguarded one. I have my hopes of the future too, but future generations are never the children of light: they are no better than those they followed, though they see different things. One is wiser to leave the future to itself: whatever else it may do, it will not fulfil our hopes in the way we anticipate. But as our personal future narrows, we become more aware of another dimension of time entirely, and may even catch glimpses of the powers and forces of a far greater creative design. Perhaps when we think we are working for the future we are really being contained in the present, though an infinite present, eternity in an hour, as Blake calls it. Perhaps too that present is also a presence, not an impersonal cause in which to lose ourselves, but a person in whom to find ourselves again. Thou art that, as the Hindus say. If the selection committee feels that I have done anything to improve the lot of mankind, I am of course very pleased. There is another kind of pleasure, however, in feeling that even in its accidents, whether of suffering or of triumph, a human life may not be "lot" at all, but a life that because it dies is a real life, a freedom that because it is known and determined is once and always free.

Thought

1. How does Frye support his claim that "there have never been any simple ages"?

2. Explain Frye's metaphor of the rear-view mirror.

3. According to Frye, what are the functions of mythology?

4. List and explain several examples of "phony mythology."

5. Do you agree with Frye's contention that "the primary motive for teaching one to read is to produce an obedient and adjusted citizen"?

6. How does Frye differentiate between "concern" and "anxiety"?

7. What do you think Frye means by "the liberalizing of the imagination"?

8. According to Frye, what societal functions does a university serve? Do you agree?

Style and Structure

9. List the allusions that Frye makes to a) people, b) places. Show how these allusions are related to Frye's central metaphor of the rear-view mirror.

Response and Extension

10. Write a reflective essay using one of the following statements as your thesis:
    a) "We think we know that the earth revolves around the sun, but we still say 'sunrise' and 'sunset' because we don't really believe it."
    b) "The humanities change just as radically as the sciences do, and on the same principles."
    c) "Man does not live directly in the world, he lives inside his own constructs of that world."
    d) "Perhaps the teacher of English sees most clearly how militant a job teaching is, and what kind of enemy it has to fight."

11. Write an editorial for your school newspaper which reflects upon the way high school should prepare students for the university as Frye sees it.

The Unspeakable State of Soliloquy

William H. Gass

- List the verbs which express aspects of talking, e.g., to preach, to mutter, to intone.
- What do the number and variety of these words indicate about the importance of talk?
- Investigate the etymology of the words "communication" and "conversation."

Dinner, let us imagine, has reached its second wine. We are exchanging pleasantries: gossip, tittle-tattle, perilously keen remarks. Like a fine sauce, they pique the mind. They pass the time. A thought is peeled and placed upon a plate. A nearby lady lends us a small smile, and there are glances brilliant as the silver. Patiently we listen while another talks, because everyone, our etiquette instructs, must have his chance to speak. We wait. We draw upon the cloth with unused knives. Our goblets turn as slowly as the world.

I want to talk to you about talking, that commonest of all our intended activities. Talking is our public link with one another: it is a need; it is an art; it is the chief instrument of all instruction; it is the most personal aspect of our private lives. To those who have sponsored our appearance in the world, the first memorable moment to follow our inaugural bawl is the awkward birth of our first word. It is that noise, a sound that is no longer a simple signal, like the squalling of a greedy gull, but a declaration of the incipient presence of mind, that delivers us into the human sphere. Before, there was only energy, intake, and excretion; now a person has begun. And in no idle, ordinary, or jesting sense, words are what that being will become. It is language which most shows a man, Ben Jonson said. "Speake that I may see thee."

To an almost measureless degree, to *know* is to possess words, and all of us who live out in the world as well as within our own are aware that we inhabit a forest of symbols; we dwell in a context of texts. Adam created the animals and birds by naming them, and we name incessantly, conserving achievements and customs, and countries that no longer exist, in the museum of human memory. But it is not only the books we pile about us like buildings, the papers we painfully compose, the exams and letters we write; it is not simply our habit of lining the streets with wheedling, hectoring, threatening signs, of turning on the radio that blats them or the TV that bumps and grinds; it is not alone the languages we learn to mispronounce, the lists, the arguments, and the rhymes we get by heart; it is not even our tendency to turn what is unwritten into writing with a mere look, so that rocks will suddenly say their age and origin and activity—no, it is not the undeniable importance of these things which leads me to lay such weight on the word. It is rather the interior self I'm concerned with, and the language that springs out of the most retired and inmost parts of us and is the image of its parent like a child: the words we use to convey our love to another, or to cope with anxiety; the words that will persuade, that will show us clearly or make the many one; the sort of words I listen to when I wait out a speech at a dinner party; words that can comfort and assuage, damage and delight, amuse and dismay. Above all, I am concerned with the words that one burns like beacons against the darkness, and that together form the society of the silently speaking self.

How desperately we need to learn to talk to ourselves. Oh, we have excellent languages for the secrets of nature. Wave packets, black holes, and skeins of genes: we can write precisely and consequentially of these, as well as other extraordinary phenomena. But can we talk of trifles: of the way a look sometimes crosses a face like the leap of a frog; of how the habit of anger raisins the heart, or wet leaves paper a street? Our anatomy texts can skin us without pain, the cellular urges of trees are no surprise, the skies are driven by winds we cannot see; yet science has passed daily life like the last bus, and left it to poetry.

It is terribly important to know how a breast is made, how to touch it to make it tingle, how to discover a hidden cyst (we find these things written of in books). But isn't it just as important to be able to put the beauty of a body into words, to communicate the self to another, and in that way form a community of feeling, of thought about feeling, of belief about thought, since there is no place for the utopia of the flesh outside the utopia of talk?

It can't be helped. We are made of layers of language like a Viennese torte. We are a Freudian dessert. Our dinner companion, the lady who lent us her smile, has raised her goblet in a quiet toast. It is as though its rim touches me, and I try to find words for the feeling, and for the wine that glows like molten rubies in her glass. If I can do that, I can take away more than a memory that will fade faster than a winter footprint; I can take away an intense and interpreted description, a record as tough to erase as a relief. Without words, what can be well and richly remembered? Yesterdays disappear like drying mist.

I remember because I talk. I talk from morning to night, and then I talk on in my sleep. Our talk is so precious to us we think we punish others when we stop. So I stay at peace because I talk. *Tête-à-têtes* are talk. Shop is talk. Parties are parades of anecdotes, gossip, opinions, raillery, and reportage. There is sometimes a band and we have to shout. Out of an incredibly complex gabble, how wonderfully clever of me to hear so immediately my own name; yet at my quiet breakfast table I may be unwilling, and thus unable, to hear a thing my wife says. When wives complain that romance has fled from their marriages, they mean their husbands have grown quiet and unresponsive as moss. Taciturnity—long, lovely word—is a famous tactic. As soon as two people decide they have nothing more to talk about, everything should be talked out. Silence shields no passion. Only the mechanical flame is sputterless and quiet.

Like a good husband, then, I tell my wife what went on through the day—in the car, on the courts, at the office. Perhaps I do not tell her *all* that went on, perhaps I give her a slightly sanitized account. I tell my friends how I fared in New York and of the impatient taxi that honked me through the streets. I tell my students the substance of what they should have read. I tell my children how it used to be (it was better), and how I was a hero (of a modest sort) in the Great War, moving from fact to fiction within the space of a single word. I tell my neighbors pleasant lies about the beauty of their lawns and dogs and vandalizing tykes, and in my head I tell the whole world where to get off.

Those who have reputations as great conversationalists are careful never to let anyone else open his mouth. Like Napoleons, they first conquer, then rule, the entire space of speech around them. Jesus preached. Samuel Johnson bullied. Carlyle fulminated. Bucky Fuller droned. Wittgenstein thought painfully aloud like a surgeon. But Socrates talked...hazardously, gaily, amorously, eloquently, religiously. He talked with wit, with passion, with honesty. He asked; he answered; he considered; he debated; he entertained; he made of his mind a boulevard before there was a France.

Talk, of course, is not always communication. It is often just a buzz, the hum a husband makes when he's still lit, but the station's gone off. We can be bores as catastrophic as quakes, causing even the earth to yawn. Talk can be cruel and injurious to a degree that is frightening: the right word wrongly used can strike a man down like a club, turn a heart dark forever, freeze the feelings. Nevertheless, while the thief is threatening to take our money or our life, he has yet to do either; and while talk mediates a strike, or weighs an allegation in the press or in committee, or considers a law in Congress, or argues a case in court, while a spouse gripes or a con man cons, while ideas are explained to a point beyond opacity by the prof, then it's not yet the dreadful day of the exam, sentence has not yet been passed, the walkout has not yet occurred. It may sound like a balk, a hitch in the motion, a failure to follow through, but many things recommend talk, not least its rich and wandering rhymes.

Our thoughts travel like our shadows in the morning walking west, casting their outlines just ahead of us so that we can see and approve, or amend and cancel, what we are about to say. This is the only rehearsal our conversations usually get. That is one reason we fall upon cliché as if it were a sofa and not a sword; for we have rehearsed bits and pieces of conversation like "Good morning" and "How are you?" and "Have a nice day" to the point where the tongue is like a stale bun in the mouth; and we have talked of Tommy's teeth and our cold car's stalling treachery, of our slobby dog's affection and Alice's asthma and Hazel's latest honeybunny, who, thank God, is only black and not gay like her last one. Indeed, it is true that prefab conversation frees the mind, yet rarely does the mind have a mind left after these clichés have conquered it. For our Gerberized phrases touch nothing; they keep the head hollow by crowding out thought; they fill all the chairs with buttocks like balloons; they are neither fed nor feed; they drift like dust; they refuse to breathe.

We forget sometimes that we live *with* ourselves—worse luck—as well as within. The head we inhabit is a haunted house. Nevertheless, we often ignore our own voice when it speaks to us: "Remember me," the spirit says. "I am your holy ghost." But we are bored by our own baloney. Why otherwise would we fall in love, if not to hear that same sweet hokum from another? Still, we should remember that we comprise true Siamese twins, fastened by language and feeling, because when we talk to ourselves we divide into the self that is all ear and the self that is all mouth. Yet which one is which? Does one self do most of the talking while the other self soaks it up, or is there a real conversation?

Frequently we put on plays, like a producer: one voice belongs to a sister, shrill and intrepidly stupid; a nephew has another (he wants a cookie); the boss is next—we've cast him as a barnyard bully; and then there is a servant or a spouse, crabby and recalcitrant. Each speaks as he or she is spoken through; each runs around in its role like a caged squirrel while an audience we have also invented (patient, visible, too easily pleased) applauds the heroine or the hero for the way he or she has righted wrongs like an avenging angel, answered every challenge like a Lancelot, every question like an Ann Landers, and met every opportunity like a perfect Romeo, every romance like a living doll. If we really love the little comedy we've constructed, it's likely to have a long run.

Does it matter how richly and honestly and well we speak? What is our attitude toward ourselves? What tone do we tend to take? Consider Hamlet, a character who escapes his circumstances and achieves greatness despite the fact that his will wavers and he can't remember the injunctions of his father's ghost. He certainly doesn't bring it off because he has an Oedipus complex (we are all supposed to have that). He is great because he talks to himself more beautifully than anyone else ever has. Consider his passion, his eloquence, his style, his range: "O what a rogue and peasant slave am I," he exclaims; "now could I drink hot blood," he brags; "to be or not to be," he wonders; "O," he hopes, "that this too too solid flesh would melt." For our part, what do *we* do? Do we lick our own hand and play the spaniel? Do we whine and wheedle, or do we natter like a ninny? Can we formulate our anger in a righteous phrase, or are we reduced to swearing like a soldier?

Many of us are ashamed to address ourselves in complete sentences. Rhetorically structured paragraphs seem pretentious, as if to gaze at our image in a mirror we had first to put on a tux. This means that everything of importance, every decision that requires care, thoughtful analysis, emotional distance, and mature judgment, must be talked out with someone else—a consequence we can't always face, with its attendant arguments, embarrassments, counterclaims, and lies. To think for yourself—not narrowly, but rather as a mind—you must be able to talk to yourself: well, honestly, and at length. You must come in from the rain of requests and responses. You must take and employ your time as if it were your life. And that side of you that speaks must be prepared to say anything so long as it is so—seen so, felt so, thought so; and that side of you that listens must be ready to hear horrors, for much of what is so *is* horrible—horrible to see, horrible to feel, horrible to consider. But at length, and honestly—that is not enough. To speak well to oneself... to speak well we must go down as far as the bucket can be lowered. Every thought must be thought through from its ultimate cost back to its cheap beginnings; every perception, however profound and distant, must be as clear and easy as the moon; every desire must be recognized as a relative and named as fearlessly as Satan named his angels. Finally, every feeling must be felt to its bottom, where the bucket rests in the silt and water rises like a tower around it. To talk to ourselves well requires, then, endless rehearsals—rehearsals in which we revise. The revision of the inner life strikes many people as hypocritical; but to think how to express some passion properly is the only way to be possessed by it. For unformed feelings lack impact, just as unfelt ideas lose weight. So walk around unrewritten, if you like. Live on broken phrases and syllable gristle, telegraphese and film reviews. No one will suspect until you speak, and your soul falls out of your mouth like a can of corn from a shelf.

There are kinds and forms of this inner speech. Many years ago, when my eldest son was about fourteen, I was gardening alongside our house one midday in mid-May, hidden between two bushes I was pruning, when Richard came out of the house in a hurry to return to school following lunch, and like a character in a French farce, skulking there, I overheard him talking to himself: "Well, racing fans, it looks... it looks like the question we've all been asking is about to be answered, because HERE COMES RICHARD GASS OUT OF THE PITS NOW. He doesn't seem to be limping from that bad crash he had at the raceway yesterday—what a crash that was!—and he is certainly going straight for his car... what courage!... his helmet is on his head, fans... yes, he is getting into his car... not a hesitation... yes, he is going to be off in a moment for the track... yes..." And then he pedaled out of my hearing, busily broadcasting his life.

Not only was my son's consciousness, in that moment, thoroughly verbal (although its subject was the Indy 500, then not too many days away), but it had a form: that given to his language and its referents by the sportscaster. As I remember it now, the verbal tone belonged more to baseball than to racing. Richard's body was, in effect, on the air; his mind was in the booth "upstairs," while his feelings were mixed with those of his audience, both at home and in the stands. He was being seen, and heard, and *spoken of*, at the same time.

This led me to wonder whether we all don't have fashions and forms in which we talk to ourselves; whether some of these might be habits of the most indelible sort, the spelling out of our secret personalities; and whether they might not vitally affect the way we speak to others, especially in our less formal moments—in bed, at breakfast, at the thirteenth tee. Might they not come from those areas of greatest influence or ambition in our lives? I recognized at once that this was true of me; that although I employed many styles and modes, there was one verbal form that had me completely in its grip. If Richard's was that of the broadcast, as it seemed, mine was that of the lecture. I realized that when I woke in the morning, I rose from bed as though at the end of a sleepless explication, already primed to ask the world if it had any questions. I was, almost from birth, and so I suppose "by nature," what Gertrude Stein called Ezra Pound: a village explainer—which, she said, was all right if you were a village, but if not, not. And sooner than sunrise I would be launched on an unvoiced speechification on the art of internal discourse, a lecture I would have given many times, though rarely aloud.

I have since asked a number of people what shape their internal talk takes, and found (when there was not a polite, amused smile which signified unalterable resistance) that they agreed to the important presence of these forms, and that one type did tend to dominate: it was often the broadcast—never the lecture—though I encountered one sermon and several prayers; it frequently took place in the courtroom where one was conducting a fearless prosecution or a triumphant defense; it was regularly the repetition of some pattern of parental exchange, a rut full of relatives and preconditioned responses; the drama appeared to be popular, as well as pornography (in this regard, there were more movies shown than words said—a pity, both modes need such improvement). There were monologues such as Browning might have penned: the vaunt, the threat, the keen, the kvetch, the eulogy for yourself when dead. There was even the bedtime story, the diary, the chronicle, and, of course, the novel, Gothic in character, or at least full of intrigue and suspense: little did William Gass realize when he rose that gentle May morning to thump his chest and touch his toes that he would soon be embarked on an adventure whose endless ramifications would utterly alter his life; otherwise he might not have set out for the supermarket without a list; otherwise he might not have done that extra push-up; he might better have stayed in bed with the bedclothes pulled over his stupidly chattering head.

Oral modes beat written ones by a mile. Obviously. They can be spoken. And the broadcast, with its apportionment of speaker into "speaker," "spectator," and "sportsman," had an edge over most of its competition. There were, finally, differences as to sex: no woman admitted she broadcast her life as though it were some sporting event.

Yet I should like to suggest (despite the undeniable sappiness of it) that the center of the self, itself, is this secret, obsessive, often silly, nearly continuous *voice*—the voice that is the surest sign we are alive; and that one fundamental function of language is the communication with this self that it makes feasible; and that if society—its families and factories and congresses and schools—has done its work, then every one of us is a bit nearer, every day, than we were before to being one of the fortunates who have made rich and beautiful the great conversation that constitutes our life.

Thought

1. Explain what Gass means by the "society of the silently speaking self."
2. According to Gass, why do people talk? Do you agree?
3. a) Why do we speak in clichés?
   b) What effects do clichés have upon individuals?
4. Why does Gass insist that one "speak well to oneself"? How important is this for you?
5. According to Gass, what is the importance of "the nearly continuous *voice*"?

Style and Structure

6. Choose several words or phrases from the essay which show that Gass loves words.
7. In what ways are the opening two paragraphs a good introduction to a reflective essay?
8. By selecting several examples from the text, show that Gass has used figurative language to make his abstractions concrete.

Response and Extension

9. Compose and perform a soliloquy which reflects upon a series of situations or events which are tied together by a common theme. Be certain to accentuate some aspects of your personality or some sudden insight into the situations.

Unit Synthesis

1. Justify the role of selfishness in the pursuit of long-term happiness by comparing the essays of Brandt and Theroux.

2. Research the influence of the 1950's on the pop culture of the 1980's. Present your findings to the class, employing as many media as possible.

3. In groups, reflect on the function of scholarship in society and in your own life. Present the results of your discussion to the class.

4. Write a short play (five to ten minutes in duration) in which several characters, who are the different sides of your personality, converse. You may wish to include some of the characters who populate your dreams.

Writing to Enthrall

The lyrical essay is intuitive and therefore unpredictable and enthralling. The authors are visionary. They write in passionate, rhapsodic styles to illuminate unusual, previously unthought-of connections among objects, ideas, and people. Frequently feelings surpass logic. As a consequence, such essays approach the poetic with their robust energy and imagistic language.

"Your dead cease to love you and the land of their nativity as soon as they pass the portals of the tomb and wander way beyond the stars. They are soon forgotten and never return," writes Chief Seattle to his oppressors. "Our dead," he continues, "never forget the beautiful world that gave them being."

Anais Nin envisions the new woman. "The woman of the future, who is really being born today, will be a woman completely free of guilt for creating and for her self-development. She will be a woman in harmony with her own strength, not necessarily called masculine, or eccentric, or something unnatural."

Camus celebrates the strength of human character, "the kind that through the virtue of its purity and sap, stands up to all the winds that blow in from the sea. Such is the strength of character that in the winter of the world will prepare the fruit."

Pablo Neruda rhapsodizes about one of the greatest English writers. Shakespeare's sonnets, he writes, "were carved from the opal of tears, from the ruby of love, from the emerald of jealousy, from the amethyst of mourning.

"They were carved from fire, made from air, sculpted from crystal."

In the lyrical essay, style becomes thought. The purpose is to enthrall.

Reply to the U.S. Government

Chief Seattle

- What assumptions do urban dwellers make about ownership of land?
- How do you think these assumptions differ from those held by Native peoples?

Yonder sky that has wept tears of compassion upon my people for centuries untold, and which to us appears changeless and eternal, may change. Today is fair. Tomorrow may be overcast with clouds. My words are like the stars that never change. Whatever Seattle says the great chief at Washington can rely upon with as much certainty as he can upon the return of the sun or the seasons. The White Chief says that Big Chief at Washington sends us greetings of friendship and goodwill. That is kind of him for we know he has little need of our friendship in return. His people are many. They are like the grass that covers vast prairies. My people are few. They resemble the scattering trees of a storm-swept plain. The great, and—I presume—good, White Chief sends us word that he wishes to buy our lands but is willing to allow us enough to live comfortably. This indeed appears just, even generous, for the Red Man no longer has rights that he need respect, and the offer may be wise also, as we are no longer in need of an extensive country.... I will not dwell on, nor mourn over, our untimely decay, nor reproach our paleface brothers with hastening it, as we too may have been somewhat to blame.

Youth is impulsive. When our young men grow angry at some real or imaginary wrong, and disfigure their faces with black paint, it denotes that their hearts are black, and then they are often cruel and relentless, and our old men and old women are unable to restrain them. Thus it has ever been. Thus it was when the white men first began to push our forefathers further westward. But let us hope that the hostilities between us may never return. We would have everything to lose and nothing to gain. Revenge by young men is considered gain, even at the cost of their own lives, but old men who stay at home in times of war, and mothers who have sons to lose, know better.

Our good father at Washington—for I presume he is now our father as well as yours, since King George has moved his boundaries further north—our great good father, I say, sends us word that if we do as he desires he will protect us. His brave warriors will be to us a bristling wall of strength, and his wonderful ships of war will fill our harbors so that our ancient enemies far to the northward—the Hydas and Tsimpsians—will cease to frighten our women, children, and old men. Then in reality will he be our father and we his children. But can that ever be? Your God is not our God! Your God loves your people and hates mine. He folds his strong and protecting arms lovingly about the paleface and leads him by the hand as a father leads his infant son—but He has forsaken His red children—if they really are his. Our God, the Great Spirit, seems also to have forsaken us. Your God makes your people wax strong every day. Soon they will fill the land. Our people are ebbing away like a rapidly receding tide that will never return. The white man's God cannot love our people or He would protect them. They seem to be orphans who can look nowhere for help. How then can we be brothers? How can your God become our God and renew our prosperity and awaken in us dreams of returning greatness? If we have a common heavenly father He must be partial—for He came to his paleface children. We never saw Him. He gave you laws but He had no word for His red children whose teeming multitudes once filled this vast continent as stars fill the firmament. No; we are two distinct races with separate origins and separate destinies. There is little common between us.

To us the ashes of our ancestors are sacred and their resting place is hallowed ground. You wander far from the graves of your ancestors and seemingly without regret. Your religion was written upon tables of stone by the iron finger of your God so that you could not forget. The Red Man could never comprehend nor remember it. Our religion is the traditions of our ancestors—the dreams of our old men, given them in solemn hours of night by the Great Spirit; and the visions of our sachems; and it is written in the hearts of our people.

Your dead cease to love you and the land of their nativity as soon as they pass the portals of the tomb and wander way beyond the stars. They are soon forgotten and never return. Our dead never forget the beautiful world that gave them being.

Day and night cannot dwell together. The Red man has ever fled the approach of the White Man, as the morning mist flees before the morning sun. However, your proposition seems fair and I think that my people will accept it and will retire to the reservation you offer them. Then we will dwell apart in peace, for the words of the Great White Chief seem to be the words of nature speaking to my people out of dense darkness.

It matters little where we pass the remnant of our days. They will not be many. A few more moons; a few more winters—and not one of the descendants of the mighty hosts that once moved over this broad land or lived in happy homes, protected by the Great Spirit, will remain to mourn over the graves of a people once more powerful and hopeful than yours. But why should I mourn at the untimely fate of my people? Tribe follows tribe, and nation follows nation, like the waves of the sea. It is the order of nature, and regret is useless. Your time of decay may be distant, but it will surely come, for even the White Man whose God walked and talked with him as friend with friend, cannot be exempt from the common destiny. We may be brothers after all. We will see.

We will ponder your proposition, and when we decide we will let you know. But should we accept it, I here and now make this condition that we will not be denied the privilege without molestation of visiting at any time the tombs of our ancestors, friends and children. Every part of this soil is sacred in the estimation of my people. Every hillside, every valley, every plain and grove, has been hallowed by some sad or happy event in days long vanished.... The very dust upon which you now stand responds more lovingly to their footsteps than to yours, because it is rich with the blood of our ancestors and our bare feet are conscious of the sympathetic touch.... Even the little children who lived here and rejoiced here for a brief season will love these somber solitudes and at eventide they greet shadowy returning spirits. And when the last Red Man shall have perished, and the memory of my tribe shall have become a myth among the White Men, these shores will swarm with the invisible dead of my tribe, and when your children's children think themselves alone in the field, the store, the shop, upon the highway, or in the silence of the pathless woods, they will not be alone.... At night when the streets of your cities and villages are silent and you think them deserted, they will throng with the returning hosts that once filled and still love this beautiful land. The White Man will never be alone.

Let him be just and deal kindly with my people, for the dead are not powerless. Dead, did I say? There is no death, only a change of worlds.

Thought

1. Identify the issue to which Chief Seattle is replying.
2. According to Chief Seattle, how are white people different from his people?
3. What future does Chief Seattle envision for his people?
4. Has history borne out his vision? Explain.

Style and Structure

5. For what purposes does Chief Seattle make extensive references to nature?
6. Show that Chief Seattle uses imagery and figurative language to enthrall the reader.

Response and Extension

7. "Every hillside, every valley, every plain and grove, has been hallowed by some sad or happy event in days long vanished...." Evoke a place that has been "hallowed" by an event in your own life, making use of imagery and figurative language where appropriate.

The New Woman

Anais Nin

- How many women can you name who are well-known as composers, sculptors or painters?
- Why are so few women well-known in these endeavours?

Why one writes is a question I can answer easily, having so often asked it of myself. I believe one writes because one has to create a world in which one can live. I could not live in any of the worlds offered to me—the world of my parents, the world of war, the world of politics. I had to create a world of my own, like a climate, a country, an atmosphere in which I could breathe, reign, and recreate myself when destroyed by living. That, I believe, is the reason for every work of art.

The artist is the only one who knows that the world is a subjective creation, that there is a choice to be made, a selection of elements. It is a materialization, an incarnation of his inner world. Then he hopes to attract others into it. He hopes to impose his particular vision and share it with others. And when the second stage is not reached, the brave artist continues nevertheless. The few moments of communion with the world are worth the pain, for it is a world for others, an inheritance for others, a gift to others in the end.

We also write to heighten our own awareness of life. We write to lure and enchant and console others. We write to serenade our lovers. We write to taste life twice, in the moment and in retrospection. We write, like Proust, to render all of it eternal, and to persuade ourselves that it is eternal. We write to be able to transcend our life, to reach beyond it. We write to teach ourselves to speak with others, to record the journey into the labyrinth. We write to expand our world when we feel strangled, or constricted, or lonely. We write as the birds sing, as the primitives dance their rituals. If you do not breathe through writing, if you do not cry out in writing, or sing in writing, then don't write, because our culture has no use for it. When I don't write, I feel my world shrinking. I feel I am in a prison. I feel I lose my fire and my color. It should be a necessity, as the sea needs to heave, and I call it breathing.

For too many centuries women have been busy being muses to the artists. And I know you have followed me in the diary when I wanted to be a muse, and I wanted to be the wife of the artist, but I was really trying to avoid the final issue—that I had to do the job myself. In letters I've received from women, I've found what Rank had described as a guilt for creating. It's a very strange illness, and it doesn't strike men— because the culture has demanded of man that he give his maximum talents. He is encouraged by the culture, to become the great doctor, the great philosopher, the great professor, the great writer. Everything is really planned to push him in that direction. Now, this was not asked of women. And in my family, just as in your family probably, I was expected simply to marry, to be a wife, and to raise children. But not all women are gifted for that, and sometimes, as D.H. Lawrence properly said, "We don't need more children in the world, we need hope."

So this is what I set out to do, to adopt all of you. Because Baudelaire told me a long time ago that in each one of us there is a man, a woman, and a child—and the child is always in trouble. The psychologists are always confirming what the poets have said so long ago. You know, even poor, maligned Freud said once, "Everywhere I go, I find a poet has been there before me." So the poet said we have three personalities, and one was the child fantasy which remained in the adult and which, in a way, makes the artist.

When I talk so much of the artist, I don't mean only the one who gives us music, who gives us color, who gives us architecture, who gives us philosophy, who gives us so much and enriches our life. I mean the creative spirit in all its manifestations. For me even as a child, when my father and mother were quarreling—my father was a pianist and my mother was a singer—when music time came, everything became peaceful and beautiful. And as children we shared the feeling that music was a magical thing which restored harmony in the family and made life bearable for us.

Now, there was a woman in France—and I give her story because it shows how we can turn and metamorphose and use everything to become creative. This was the mother of Utrillo. Because she was very poor, the mother of Utrillo was condemned to be a laundress and a houseworker. But she lived in Montmartre at the time of almost the greatest group of painters that was ever put together, and she became a model for them. As she watched the painters paint, she learned to paint. And she became, herself, a noted painter, Suzanne Valadon. It was the same thing that happened to me when I was modelling at the age of sixteen, because I didn't have any profession and I didn't know how else to earn a living. I learned from the painters the sense of color, which was to train me in observation my whole life.

I learned many things from the artist which I would call creating out of nothing. Varda, for example, taught me that collage is made out of little bits of cloth. He even had me cut a piece of the lining of my coat because he took a liking to the color of it and wanted to incorporate it into a collage. He was making very beautiful celestial gardens and fantasies of every possible dream with just little bits of cloth and glue. Varda is also the one who taught me that if you leave a chair long enough on the beach, it becomes bleached into the most beautiful color imaginable which you could never find with paint.

I learned from Tinguely that he went to junkyards, and he picked out all kinds of bits and pieces of machines and built some machines which turned out to be caricatures of technology. He even built a machine which committed suicide, which I described in a book called *Collages*. I am trying to say that the artist is a magician—that he taught me that no matter where you are put, you can always somehow come out of that place.

Now, I was placed somewhere you might imagine would be terribly interesting, a suburb of Paris. But a suburb of Paris can be just as lonely as a suburb of New York or Los Angeles or San Francisco. I was in my twenties and I didn't know anyone at the time, so I turned to my love of writers. I wrote a book, and suddenly I found myself in a Bohemian, artistic, literary writer's world. And that was my bridge. But sometimes, when people say to me, that's fine, but you were gifted for writing, my answer is that there is not always that kind of visible skill.

I know a woman who started with nothing, whom I consider a great heroine. She had not been able to go to high school because her family was very poor and had so many children. The family lived on a farm in Saratoga, but she decided to go to New York City. She began working at Brentano's and after a little while told them that she wanted to have a bookshop of her own. They laughed at her and said that she was absolutely mad and would never survive the summer. She had $150 saved and she rented a little place that went downstairs in the theater section of New York, and everybody came in the evening after the theater. And today her bookshop is not only the most famous bookshop in New York, the Gotham Book Mart, but it is a place where everybody wants to have bookshop parties. She has visitors from all over the world—Edith Sitwell came to see her when she came to New York, Jean Cocteau, and many more. And no other bookshop in New York has that fascination, which comes from her, her humanity and friendliness, and the fact that people can stand there and read a book and she won't even notice them. Frances Steloff is her name, and I mention her whenever anyone claims that it takes a particular skill to get out of a restricted, limited, or impoverished life. Frances is now eighty-six, a beautiful old lady with white hair and perfect skin who has defied age.

It was the principle of creative will that I admired and learned from musicians like Eric Satie, who defied starvation and used his compositions to protect his piano from the dampness of his little room in a suburb of Paris. Even Einstein, who disbelieved Newton's unified field theory, died believing what is being proved now. I give that as an instance of faith, and faith is what I want to talk about. What kept me writing, when for twenty years I was received by complete silence, is that faith in the necessity to be the artist—and no matter what happens even if there is no one listening.

I don't need to speak of Zelda Fitzgerald. I think all of you have thought about Zelda, how she might never have lost her mind if Fitzgerald had not forbidden her to publish her diary. It is well known that Fitzgerald said no, that it could not be published, because he would need it for his own work. This, to me, was the beginning of Zelda's disturbance. She was unable to fulfill herself as a writer and was overpowered by the reputation of Fitzgerald. But if you read her own book, you will find that in a sense she created a much more original novel than he ever did, one more modern in its effort to use language in an original way.

History, much like the spotlight, has hit whatever it wanted to hit, and very often it missed the woman. We all know about Dylan Thomas. Very few of us know about Caitlin Thomas, who after her husband's death wrote a book which is a poem in itself and sometimes surpasses his own—in strength, in primitive beauty, in a real wakening of feeling. But she was so overwhelmed by the talent of Dylan Thomas that she never thought anything of her writing at all until he died.

So we're here to celebrate the sources of faith and confidence. I want to give you the secrets of the constant alchemy that we must practice to turn brass into gold, hate into love, destruction into creation—to change the crass daily news into inspiration, and despair into joy. None need misinterpret this as indifference to the state of the world or to the actions by which we can stem the destructiveness of the corrupt system. There is an acknowledgement that, as human beings, we need nourishment to sustain the life of the spirit, so that we can act in the world, but I don't mean turn away. I mean we must gain our strength and our values from self-growth and self-discovery. Against all odds, against all handicaps, against the chamber of horrors we call history, man has continued to dream and to depict its opposite. That is what we have to do. We do not escape into philosophy, psychology, and art—we go there to restore our shattered selves into whole ones.

The woman of the future, who is really being born today, will be a woman completely free of guilt for creating and for her self-development. She will be a woman in harmony with her own strength, not necessarily called masculine, or eccentric, or something unnatural. I imagine she will be very tranquil about her strength and her serenity, a woman who will know how to talk to children and to the men who sometimes fear her. Man has been uneasy about this self-evolution of woman, but he need not be—because, instead of having a dependent, he will have a partner. He will have someone who will not make him feel that every day he has to go into battle against the world to support a wife and child, or a childlike wife. The woman of the future will never try to live vicariously through the man, and urge and push him to despair, to fulfill something that she should really be doing herself. So that is my first image—she is not aggressive, she is serene, she is sure, she is confident, she is able to develop her skills, she is able to ask for space for herself.

I want this quality of the sense of the person, the sense of direct contact with human beings to be preserved by woman, not as something bad, but as something that could make a totally different world where intellectual capacity would be fused with intuition and with a sense of the personal.

Now, when I wrote the diary and when I wrote fiction, I was trying to say that we need both intimacy and a deep knowledge of a few human beings. We also need mythology and fiction which is a little further away, and art is always a little further away from the entirely personal world of the woman. But I want to tell you the story of Colette. When her name was suggested for the Académie française, which is considered the highest honor given to writers, there was much discussion because she hadn't written about war, she hadn't written about any large event, she had only written about love. They admired her as a writer, as a stylist—she was one of our best stylists—but somehow the personal world of Colette was not supposed to have been very important. And I think it is extremely important, because we have lost that intimacy and that person-to-person sense, which she developed because she had been more constricted and less active in the world. So the family was very important, the neighbor was very important, and the friend was very important.

It would be nice if men could share that too, of course. And they will, on the day they recognize the femininity in themselves, which is what

Jung has been trying to tell us. I was asked once how I felt about men who cried, and I said that I loved men who cried, because it showed they had feeling. The day that woman admits what we call her masculine qualities, and man admits his so-called feminine qualities, will mean that we admit we are androgynous, that we have many personalities, many sides to fulfill. A woman can be courageous, can be adventurous, she can be all these things. And this new woman who is coming up is very inspiring, very wonderful. And I love her.

Thought

1. Discuss and evaluate Nin's assertion that "the artist is the only one who knows that the world is a subjective creation."
2. Why do some women suffer "the guilt for creating"?
3. Have Nin's illustrations convincingly demonstrated her contention that "we do not escape into philosophy, psychology, and art—we go there to restore our shattered selves into whole ones"?
4. Describe the woman of the future as Nin envisions her.
5. Why is the new woman "very inspiring, very wonderful" to Nin? Do you agree?

Style and Structure

6. What stylistic devices has Nin used to make this essay lyrical in tone?
7. Does the author's voice intrude upon the thought of the essay? Explain.

Response and Extension

8. Write a lyrical essay which expresses your feelings about the "new man" who would be the perfect complement to the "new woman."
9. In your journal, write about someone who has influenced your creative spirit.

The Almond Trees

Albert Camus

● Under what circumstances is the use of force justified?
● What is the best strategy to use in resisting force?

"Do you know," Napoleon once said to Fontanes, "what astounds me most about the world? The impotence of force to establish anything. There are only two powers in the world: the sword and the mind. In the end, the sword is always conquered by the mind."

Conquerors, you see, are sometimes melancholy. They have to pay some price for so much vainglory. But what a hundred years ago was true of the sword is no longer true today of the tank. Conquerors have made progress, and the dismal silence of places without intelligence has been established for years at a time in a lacerated Europe. At the time of the hideous wars of Flanders, Dutch painters could still perhaps paint the cockerels in their farmyards. The Hundred Years War has likewise been forgotten, and yet the prayers of Silesian mystics still linger in some hearts. But today, things have changed; the painter and the monk have been drafted—we are one with the world. The mind has lost that regal certainty which a conqueror could acknowledge; it exhausts itself now in cursing force, for want of knowing how to master it.

Some noble souls keep on deploring this, saying it is evil. We do not know if it is evil, but we know it is a fact. The conclusion is that we must come to terms with it. All we need know, then, is what we want. And what we want precisely is never again to bow beneath the sword, never again to count force as being in the right unless it is serving the mind.

The task is endless, it's true. But we are here to pursue it. I do not have enough faith in reason to subscribe to a belief in progress or to any philosophy of history. I do believe at least that man's awareness of his destiny has never ceased to advance. We have not overcome our condition, and yet we know it better. We know that we live in contradiction, but we also know that we must refuse this contradiction and do what is needed to reduce it. Our task as men is to find the few principles that will calm the infinite anguish of free souls. We must mend what has been torn apart, make justice imaginable again in a world so obviously unjust, give happiness a meaning once more to peoples poisoned by the misery of the century. Naturally, it is a superhuman task. But superhuman is the term for tasks men take a long time to accomplish, that's all.

Let us know our aims then, holding fast to the mind, even if force puts on a thoughtful or a comfortable face in order to seduce us. The first thing is not to despair. Let us not listen too much to those who proclaim that the world is at an end. Civilizations do not die so easily, and even if our world were to collapse, it would not have been the first. It is indeed true that we live in tragic times. But too many people confuse tragedy with despair. "Tragedy," Lawrence said, "ought to be a great kick at misery." This is a healthy and immediately applicable thought. There are many things today deserving such a kick.

When I lived in Algiers, I would wait patiently all winter because I knew that in the course of one night, one cold, pure February night, the almond trees of the Vallée des Consuls would be covered with white flowers. I would marvel then at the sight of this fragile snow resisting the rains and the wind from the sea. Yet every year it lasted just long enough to prepare the fruit.

There is no symbol here. We will not win our happiness with symbols. We'll need something more solid. I mean only that sometimes, when life weighs too heavily today in a Europe still full of misery, I turn toward those shining lands where so much strength is still intact. I know them too well not to realize that they are the chosen land where courage and contemplation can live in harmony. Thinking of them teaches me that if we are to save the mind we must ignore its gloomy virtues and celebrate its strength and wonder. Our world is poisoned by its misery, and seems to wallow in it. It has utterly surrendered to that evil which Nietzsche called the spirit of heaviness. Let us not add to this. It is futile to weep over the mind, it is enough to labor for it.

But where are the conquering virtues of the mind? The same Nietzsche listed them as mortal enemies to heaviness of the spirit. For him, they are strength of character, taste, the "world," classical happiness, severe pride, the cold frugality of the wise. More than ever, these virtues are necessary today, and each of us can choose the one that suits him best. Before the vastness of the undertaking, let no one forget strength of character. I don't mean the theatrical kind on political platforms, complete with frowns and threatening gestures. But the kind that through the virtue of its purity and its sap, stands up to all the winds that blow in from the sea. Such is the strength of character that in the winter of the world will prepare the fruit.

Thought

1. According to Camus, what major change has occurred to the mind since Napoleon's time?
2. In the author's view, what is the task of humanity? Do you agree
3. What place do the almond trees occupy in the author's thought
4. What are the "conquering virtues of the mind"?
5. Which of the "conquering virtues" do you think is the most necessary to the world today?

Style and Structure

6. What stylistic use has Camus made of the quotations from Napoleon and Lawrence?
7. What stylistic purpose is served by the almond trees?

Response and Extension

8. Select an image from the natural world. Write a lyrical essay expressing your feelings about this image. Be certain to show the relationship between this image and your thought.
9. Select a piece of music which you think is lyrical. Write a poem to accompany this piece of music.

Shakespeare, Prince of Light

Pablo Neruda

- Why do people read and perform Shakespeare's plays some 400 years after his birth?

Goneril, Regan, Hamlet, Angus, Duncan, Glansdale, Mortimer, Ariel, Leontes...

These names from Shakespeare were part of our childhood; they crystallized and became the substance of our dreams. Even when we could scarcely read, we knew that behind the names lay a continent with rivers and kings, clans and castles and archipelagos, that someday we would explore. The names of these somber, or radiant, protagonists revealed to us the texture of poetry, the first peal of a great bell. Later, much later, come the days and years when we discover the lines and lives of these names. We discover suffering and remorse, martyrdom and cruelty, beings of blood, creatures of air, voices illuminated for a magic feast, banquets attended by bloodstained ghosts. All that action, all those souls, all those passions—all that life.

In every epoch, one bard assumes responsibility for the dreams and the wisdom of the age: he expresses the growth, the expansion, of that world. His name is Alighieri, Victor Hugo, Lope de Vega, Walt Whitman.

Above all, his name is Shakespeare.

These bards amass leaves, and among the leaves one hears birdcalls; beneath these leaves roots grow. They are the leaves of great trees.

They are leaves, and eyes. They multiply and gaze down on us, insignificant men, through all the passing ages, they gaze on us and help us discover ourselves: they reveal to us our labyrinths.

In the case of Shakespeare, there is a third revelation, as there will be others: that of the sorcery of his distilled poetry. Few poets are so compact and secret, so secure in the heart of their diamond.

The sonnets were carved from the opal of tears, from the ruby of love, from the emerald of jealousy, from the amethyst of mourning.

They were carved from fire, made from air, sculpted from crystal.

The sonnets were uprooted from nature so whole that, from first to last, one hears how water flows, how the wind dances, and how, golden or flowering, the cycles of the seasons and fruits follow one after the other.

The sonnets hold an infinity of keys, of magic formulas: static majesty, speeding arrows.

The sonnets are banners that one by one rise to flutter from the castle tower. And though exposed to weather and to time, they conserve the magenta of their stars, the turquoise of their half-moons, the splendor of their blazing hearts.

I have read Shakespeare's poetry for many years; the poems, unlike the plays, do not tell of lives, of battles, of derring-do.

There is the stark whiteness of the page, the purity of the road of poetry. Along that road glide endless rows of images, like tiny ships laden with honey.

Amid this excess of riches in which the driving power of creativity moves in time with intelligence, we see, we can almost feel, an unwavering and flourishing Shakespeare, and note that the most striking aspect of his poems is not their abundant power but their exacting form.

My name is written in my copy of the *Sonnets*, along with the day and the month in 1930 when I bought the book on the island of Java.

It has been with me, then, for thirty-four years.

There, on that far-off island, it was my model, the purest of fountains, deep forests, a fabulous multitude of hitherto unknown myths; it was crystalline law. Because Shakespeare's poetry, like that of Góngora and Mallarmé, plays with the light of reason, imposes a strict, if secret, code. In a word, during those lost years of my life, Shakespeare's poetry kept open a line of communication with Western culture. By Western, naturally, I mean Pushkin and Karl Marx, Bach and Hölderlin, Lord Tennyson and Mayakovsky.

Of course, poetry recurs throughout the plays as well, in the towers of Elsinore, in the castle of Macbeth, on Prospero's ship, among the perfume of pomegranates in Verona.

A phantasmagorical wind blows through the tunnel of each play. The oldest sound in the world, the sound of the human heart, is the matter from which these unforgettable words are formed. Fantasy and humanity appear in all the plays, along with the parlance of the common man, the signs of the marketplace, the vulgar voices of parasites and buffoons, all accompanied by the steely ring of suits of armor locked in crazed combat.

But what I like best is to follow the extravagant flow of Shakespeare's poetry, a harmony painted on the wall of time in blue, enamel, and magic seafoam, an amalgam imprinted on our eternity.

As an example, in the pastoral idyll *Venus and Adonis*, published in 1593, there is the flickering of cool shadows on flowing waters, the insinuating green of singing groves, cascades of rippling poetry, and myth fleeing into the greenery.

Then suddenly a steed appears, dissipating fantasy with its pounding hoofs, as "His eye, which scornfully glisters like fire, shows his hot courage and his high desire."

Yes, if a painter were to paint that horse: "His art with nature's workmanship at strife, as if the dead the living should exceed." There is no description that can equal that of this amorous, furious horse galloping with real hoofs through marvelous sextets.

And I mention it, though Shakespeare's bestiary contained traces of many beasts, and his herbarium retains the color and scent of many flowers, because that pawing steed is the theme of his ode, the generative force of nature captured by a great synthesizer of dreams.

This autumn I was given the task of translating *Romeo and Juliet*.

I accepted the request with humility. With humility, and with a sense of duty, because in fact I did not feel capable of decanting that passionate love story into Spanish. But I had to do it, since this is the anniversary of Shakespeare's birth, the year of universal veneration of the poet who opened new universes to man.

Translating with pleasure, and with honor, the tragedy of those star-crossed lovers, I made a discovery.

I realized that underlying the plot of undying love and inescapable death there was a second drama, a second subject, a second principal theme.

Romeo and Juliet is a great plea for peace among men. It is a condemnation of pointless hatred, a denunciation of the barbarity of war, and the solemn consecration of peace.

When Prince Escalus, in moving and exemplary language, reproaches the feudal clans who are staining the streets of Verona with blood, we realize that the Prince is the incarnation of enlightenment, of dignity, and of peace.

When Benvolio reproaches Tybalt for his warlike temperament, saying: "I do but keep the peace; put up thy sword," the fierce swordsman replies: "What! drawn, and talk of peace? I hate the word..."

So, peace was despised by some in Elizabethan Europe. Centuries later, Gabriela Mistral—persecuted and insulted for her defense of peace, dismissed from the Chilean newspaper that had published her articles for thirty years—wrote her famous phrase: "Peace, that accursed word." One sees that the world and the press continued to be governed by Tybalts, by swordsmen.

One reason more, then, to love William Shakespeare, the greatest of all human beings. There will always be time and space to explore in Shakespeare, to lose ourselves, or begin the long journey around his statue, like the Lilliputians around Gulliver. And though we may go a long way without reaching the end, we always return with hands filled with fragrance and blood, with flowers and sorrows, with mortal treasures.

At this solemn moment, it is my pleasure to open the door of tributes, raising the curtain so the dazzling, pensive figure of the Bard may appear. And across four centuries I would say to him: "Greetings, Prince of Light! Good health, sir itinerant actor! We are the heirs to your great dreams; we dream them still. Your words do honor to the entire world."

And, more quietly, I would whisper into his ear: "My friend, I thank you."

Thought

1. According to Neruda, in what does the greatness of Shakespeare lie?
2. What discovery has Neruda made about *Romeo and Juliet?* Do you agree with him?
3. Why is Neruda impressed with the character of Escalus?
4. Do you agree that the world is "governed by Tybalts, by swordsmen"?

Style and Structure

5. Select three examples of each of Neruda's a) poetic diction, b) figurative language, c) unusual syntax. Show how these elements contribute to the lyrical nature of the essay.
6. What is Neruda's purpose in writing this essay?

Response and Extension

7. Using Neruda's essay as your model, write a lyrical essay praising the artistic and human qualities of the artist you most admire.
8. Debate the following statement: "The driving power of creativity moves in time with intelligence."

Unit Synthesis

1. By referring to all of the writers in this chapter, write a lyrical essay which celebrates the human spirit.

2. Compare the tone of Nin's essay with that of one of the other essays which addresses women's issues.

3. Read a novel by Albert Camus, such as *The Stranger, The Plague,* or *The Fall.* Write a critical essay which examines the degree to which the thought contained in his essay, "The Almond Trees," is consistent with the novel.

4. Read a collection of poems by Pablo Neruda such as *The Captain's Verses, Residence on Earth,* or *Twenty Love Poems and a Song of Despair.* Rehearse several poems for a reading which you perform for your class.

5. Read Pablo Neruda's *Memoirs* or the diaries of Anais Nin.

6. Write a book review of one of the following: *Bury My Heart at Wounded Knee* by Dee Brown; *I Heard the Owl Call My Name* by Margaret Craven; *Klee Wyck* by Emily Carr; *The Moccasin Telegraph* by W.P. Kinsella; or *Dreamspeaker* by Cam Hubert.

CONTENTS BY THEME

Morals and Ethics

Relationships

Science and Technology

CONTENTS BY FORM

Articles

Speeches

Policy Statement

Prentice-Hall Canada Inc., Secondary School Division, and the editors of *Essays: Thought and Style* are committed to the publication of instructional materials that are as bias-free as possible. This anthology was evaluated for bias prior to publication.

The editors and publisher also recognize the importance of appropriate reading levels and have therefore made every effort to ensure the highest degree of readability in the student text. The content has been selected, organized, and written at a level suitable to the intended audience. Standard readability tests have been applied to ensure an appropriate reading level.

Research indicates, however, that readability is affected by much more than word or sentence length; factors such as presentation, format and design, none of which are considered in the usual readability tests, also greatly influence the ease with which students read a book. These and many additional features have been carefully prepared to ensure maximum student comprehension.

Acknowledgements

Page 2   From EACH MOMENT AS IT FLIES by Harry Bruce. Methuen Publications, 1984. Used by permission.

Page 5   From PIECES OF EIGHT by Sydney J. Harris. Copyright ©1975, 1976, 1977, 1978, 1979, 1980, 1981 by The Chicago Daily News, The Chicago Sun-Times, Field Newspaper Syndicate and Sydney J. Harris. Copyright ©1982 by Houghton Mifflin Company. Reprinted by permission of Houghton Mifflin Company.

Page 8   Reprinted from *Ms. Magazine*, March 1980, with permission.

Page 12   Copyright ©1980 by Woody Allen. Reprinted from SIDE EFFECTS, by Woody Allen, by permission of Random House, Inc.

Page 18   From HEART OF A STRANGER by Margaret Laurence. Used by permission of The Canadian Publishers, McClelland and Stewart Limited, Toronto.

Page 24   From BIOPHILIA by Edward O. Wilson. Harvard University Press, 1984. Copyright ©1984 by the President and Fellows of Harvard College. Reprinted by permission.

Page 30   "The Seven Wonders," from LATE NIGHT THOUGHTS ON LISTENING TO MAHLER'S NINTH SYMPHONY, by Lewis Thomas. Copyright ©1983 by Lewis Thomas. Reprinted by permission of Viking Penguin, Inc.

Page 36   From SATURDAY NIGHT, October 1986. Reprinted by permission.

Page 40   From YOU MAY KNOW THEM AS SEA URCHINS, MA'AM: WRITINGS BY RAY GUY. Breakwater Books Ltd., 1975. Reprinted by permission.

Page 46   From ESQUIRE, 1984. Reprinted by permission.

Page 51   From *The Enthusiasms of Robertson Davies*, edited by Judith Skelton Grant. Used by permission of The Canadian Publishers, McClelland and Stewart Limited, Toronto.

Page 56   "Marriage is Belonging" is excerpted from the book THE COLLECTED ESSAYS AND OCCASIONAL WRITINGS OF KATHERINE ANNE PORTER. Copyright ©1951 by Katherine Anne Porter. Originally published in MADEMOISELLE. Reprinted by permission of DELACORTE PRESS/SEYMOUR LAWRENCE.